SP

Bo

Cairngorms National Park
Loch Lomond National Park

Buy on line at
www.cairngormslivingwalks.com

Living Walks
in the Cairngorms National Park

Living Walks is published By

Ice Publishing
Aviemore/Kincraig
icep@btopenworld.com
www.cairngormslivingwalks.com

Walked by: Tony Brown & Brac
Compiled by: Tony Brown
Design & Layout: Tony Brown
Editorial: Tom Ramage

Photography
Ynot
The cover picture was chosen by
the Waterstones team in Aviemore
(what stars!).

Special thanks to our sponsors, without
whom this book would not have been
possible (see outside back cover)

Maps
Ordnance Survey
CrownCopyright Licence N0 100048399.
Maps In Minutes.

First Published: February 2009
ISBN 978-1-900916-20-2

Cairngorms National Park
125 Living Walks

Contents

Introduction		3
Maps & web site		8
Getting Around		10
Featured Walks at a Glance		12
Angus Glens		16
Aviemore & Glenmore		50
Ballater, Braemar & Dinnet		86
Boat of Garten, Carrbridge Grantown-on-Spey & Nethy Bridge		132
Glenlivet / Tomintoul & Strathdon		196
Kincraig & Kingussie		224
Laggan & Newtonmore		262
Walked it		286
Walking Services		308
Dog Owners	312,	314
Index		316
Scottish Outdoor Access Code		317

Introduction by Tony Brown

Welcome to the high road:
you are in Britain's
"top" national park:

If you live to walk,
Living Walks is for you!

To the tenderfoot we aim to introduce some of the fairest routes in the Cairngorms, and with the time-served explorer we aim to share some of the most rewarding.

This guide is packed with dozens of trails for all, but the emphasis is on the large number of interesting family routes there are, in and around the towns and villages of the largest and most diverse of our national parks.

The idea wasn't actually mine. It was prompted by hill-walkers themselves - having published three other guides in the Spot On series, I was avalanched! Initially I considered there were already plenty of walking books and resisted, but when I actually started looking into them I was surprised to learn just how little information there was for 'normal' walkers.

Visit any bookshop or tourist office and you will see shelves stacked with volumes for hill-walkers and summit-conquerors, but nothing for you and me. Virtually all the guide-books are aimed at hard-core trekkers on a mission, there is little or no information provided for people wanting to do short, easy family walks. However, some estates, landowners, outdoor centres and villages do provide good local information.

After some thought I decided to compile a walking guide, but I wasn't going to invent new walks: I decided to focus on the many existing marked out trails dotted all

Loch Brandy Walk
Glen Clova

around the Cairngorms, from Aviemore down to the Angus Glens. I wanted to concentrate on outings which would appeal to the casual walker or a real newcomer, someone who'd never been on a leisure walk at all.

Brac

There are over 125 routes in this guide. With my trusty dog Brac, the mad golden retriever, I have walked every single one. We started off in Aviemore and finished with the trails around Royal Deeside, and over eight weeks the two of us covered more than 360 miles, negotiating fields, hilltops, river-crossings, forests and mountains. (For every mile we walked I'm donating £1 to Children in Need, the charity dedicated to raising awareness of and supporting vulnerable kids. Perhaps you to may want to donate to a charity, to mark each walk you complete).

Key to walking symbols

- Walk Orientation
- Walk Length
- Walk Grade
- Walk Time
- Walk Height Gain
- Walk Hills & Steeps
- Walk Terrain
- Walk Route Marks
- Walk for Wheelchairs
- Walk Access for Prams
- Key Walk Features
- Walk View points
- Water Features
- Dog Walking Guide
- Parking
- Public Toilets
- Local Facilities
- Good Family Walk

Introduction

From the outset it was clear just how many fantastic walks there are in the Cairngorms. What also became clear was just how little public exposure there is regarding their awesome diversity. I had no idea how efficiently so many of them are marked out. For instance, the quality of way-marking on the walks managed by the Forestry Commission at Glenmore, near Aviemore, and the Cambus O May Forest Trails near Ballater is truly superb, with a walk to suit everyone of every age.

Once I had finished all the walks I soon identified my favourites, which range from the superb treks in the Glen Doll Forest in Glen Clova to the trails around Braemar, such as the one around Craig Leek, and the unusual trail known as the Lion's Face and the

Cromlins near Braemar Castle. Among the most stunning features I discovered were the marked trails at the Uath Lochans in the Glenfeshie area near Kincraig.

Some think that walking in the countryside is the preserve of a few anoraks, bound by some unwritten code to suffer dull clothes, silly hats, maps wrapped in cling film worn around the neck and - the very latest must-have walking accessory - collapsible ski poles...

Well forget it, it's all hype and you don't need overpriced clothes or fancy gizmos. Nor do you need to have a name tag on your jacket and be led by a team leader clad in ill-fitting fatigues. All you really need is a sense of humour and a desire for some fun and outdoor adventure. However, on a serious note, always match your attire to suit the area, terrain and the weather. You will read in books and on websites that you are advised to wear suitable clothing and footwear for this or that walk, but frankly it's common sense. Check the forecast, and if it is raining before you head out then take a good weatherproof jacket; likewise, if you are going to be walking in the open countryside, and in particular the Scottish Highlands, then good footwear is obvious, but to stress this or that footwear for a particular walk is not always possible, given that on a dry day a pair of trainers may be fine for some of the low level trails, while the following day the same walk may require sturdy water-proof boots due to a downpour of rain, or a heavy snowstorm, so use common sense and simply avoid trouble. Whatever your footwear, waterproof is best.

For simple family walks, what you don't need to do is spend vast sums of money on walking aids like sat-nav paraphernalia, however where there is no room for complacency is on walks that take you out to the back of beyond up on mountains and over hills: this is when the specialist gear is needed and you have to kit up with the works. Never go out unprepared and, if in doubt, consult a specialist. You should never head out without a map and compass and the skill to use them! And no matter where you walk, it's always a good idea to inform someone of your exact plans - leave details where they can be found, noting times, routes and who's in the group.

Nino on tour with Abby

Apart from a couple, all the walks listed are way-marked - this means the routes have been plotted with colour markers or number posts, which you simply follow as you go. However, as you are venturing into the countryside it's always a good idea to have a map to follow, regardless of what markers there are. This way you can plot your route and get a good sense of where you are. Large maps for each walk can be found on our new Living Walks web site (see next the page for details).

Introduction - Maps & Web Site

MAPS

Regarding maps in this book: we have included small sections for each walk to help you get an idea and the orientation. However, we decided not to include large maps in a small book because of the number of pages they would take up. But you can now get a large walker-friendly map from our new website:

Here you will find sections of Ordnance Survey Explore maps, each trail marked out with walking data. Once you have logged on you can download a walk-friendly map and print it off as often as you want, free of charge.

www.cairngormslivingwalks.com

Maps - by permission of Ordnance Survey CrownCopyright Licence N0 100048399

Please note: while I have tried to include all the relevant data for each walk as I found it, landowners always reserve the right to make changes to walking routes and posted signs or markers, so trails may differ to what you read in this book or on the Internet. Another factor to note is that marker posts can often become dislodged due to harsh weather, wear and tear and even livestock, so always check with landowners before setting off to ensure that a path is open.

Finally: now my feet and Brac's paws have been restored, I can't stress enough just how much I enjoyed the walks, and all those who know me are well aware that I am as far from being a walker as it gets. But doing this book has been a real eye-opener and I will definitely be out there doing the walks again with not only Brac, but my son Bruce and daughter Cara.

Cara taking a walk in the park

Tony & Brac

Dad's special girl.

Getting Around.

DISTANCE BETWEEN VILLAGES

Aviemore to Carrbridge	= 6 miles
Carrbridge to Boat of Garten	= 4 miles
Boat of Garten to Nethy Bridge	= 4 miles
Nethy Bridge to Dulnain Bridge	= 3 miles
Grantown to Tomintoul	= 14 miles
Tomintoul to Glenlivet	= 9 miles
Tomintoul to Strathdon	= 18 miles
Strathdon to Dinnet	= 15 miles
Dinnet to Ballater	= 7 miles
Ballater to Angus Glens	= 40 miles
Ballater to Braemar	= 16 miles
Braemar to Dalwhinnie	= 68 miles
Dalwhinnie to Laggan	= 7 miles
Laggan to Newtonmore	= 7 miles
Newtonmore to Kingussie	= 4 miles
Kingussie to Kincraig	= 6 miles
Kincraig to Aviemore	= 6 miles

Tourist Information Offices
and villages with fuel services

- 𝑖 🅿 Aviemore
- 𝑖 🅿 Ballater
- 𝑖 🅿 Braemar
- 🅿 Carrbridgee
- 🅿 Dalwhinnie
- 𝑖 Kingussie
- 𝑖 🅿 Grantown-on-Spey
- 𝑖 🅿 Newtonmore
- 𝑖 Tomintoul

www.visitscotland.com
tel 0845 22 55 121

Lost in the park!! Joy, Becky & Sam

Walks around the Park:

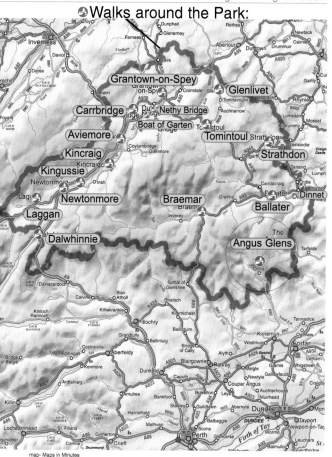

map- Maps in Minutes

Featured Walks at a Glance

● Easy　● Moderate　● Challenging　🖾 Good Family Walk - (1) = 1 Way - (R) = Return

WALK	GRADE	DISTANCE	TIME	PAGE
Angus Glens				
Glendoll Forest Walk	●	3 miles	1½ hours	22
Invermark Castle to Loch Lee	●	4.4 miles	2 hours (R)	24
Invermark to Queens Well	●	5 miles	3 hours (R)	26
Loch Brandy Walk	●	3 miles	2 hours (R)	28
South Esk Loop & Trout Loch	●	2.5 miles	1 hour	30
South Esk River Walk	●	2 miles	1 hour	32
The Dounalt Walk	●	5 miles	2½ hours	34
The Minister's Path	●	6 miles (1)	3 hours	36
Walk up to Corrie Fee Reserve	●	4 miles	2 hours	38
White Water Trail	●	2.5 miles	1½ hours	40
Aviemore & Glenmore				
Allt Mor All Abilities Trail	● 🖾	400 metres	20 minutes	50
Allt Mor to Cairngorms	●	3.5 miles	2 hours (1)	52
Aviemore Orbital Path	● 🖾	2 miles	1 hour	54
Aviemore Speyside Golf Walk	●	4.5 miles	2 hours	56
Aviemore to Boat of Garten	●	6 miles	2½ hours	58
Coire Cas Lower Loop	●	3/4 mile	45 minutes	60
Coylumbridge to the Iron Bridge	●	4.5 miles	2 hours	62
Craigellachie Nature Reserve Trails	● 🖾	2 miles	1 hour	64
Glenmore Forest Trail	● 🖾	3 miles	1½ hours	66
Lilly Loch Walk	● 🖾	3 miles	1½ hours	68
Loch an Eilein Trail Circular	● 🖾	3 miles	1½ hours	70
Loch Morlich Circular	●	3.4 miles	1½ hours	72
Loch nan Carriagen Stone Circle	● 🖾	2 miles	50 minutes	74
Lochan Nan Nathrach Trail	●	3.4 miles	1½ hours	76
Loch Vaa	● 🖾	1.5 miles	50 minutes	78
Ryvoan & Green Loch Trex	●	4.4 miles	2 hours	80
The Queens Forest Walk	●	4.4 miles	2 hours	82
The Woodland Trail	● 🖾	1 mile	50 minutes	84
Ballater, Braemar & Dinnet				
Ballater area				
Ballater Golf Course Walk	● 🖾	2 miles	1 hour	94

WALK	GRADE	DISTANCE	TIME	PAGE
Craigendarroch Walk	●	2 miles	1½ hours	96
Lock Muick End View Circular	●	2.5 miles	1½ hours	98
Pannanich Woods	●	3 miles	1½ hours	100
Seven Bridges Walk	●	5 miles	2 hours	102
Braemar area				
Around Craig Leek	◉	5.2 miles	2½ hours	104
Keiloch Crag	●	3 miles	1½ hours	106
Morrone Birkwood	●	3 miles	1½ hours	108
Morrone Hill Walk	●	6 miles	3 hours	110
Queen's Drive Walk	●	3 miles	1½ hours	112
River Dee Walk	◉	3 miles	1½ hours	114
The Creag Choinnich Walk	●	2 miles	1½ hours	116
The Lion's Face & Cromlins	●	2.5 miles	1½ hours	118
Dinnet area				
Burn O'Vat Circular	●	1.3 miles	45 minutes	120
Cambus O May Forest Trails	●	3 mile (L)	Various	122
Cambus O May Bridge Walk	●	2.25 miles	1¼ hours	124
Glen Tanar Nature Reserve	●	5 miles (L)	2½ hours	126
Little Ord Circular	●	1.8 miles	1 hour	128
Loch Kinord Circular	●	5.3 miles	2½ hours	130
Boat of Garten, Carrbridge, Grantown & Nethy Bridge				
Boat of Garten area				
Boat of Garten to Carrbridge	●	5 miles	2½ hours	142
Boat of Garten to Loch Vaa	●	2.5 miles	1½ hours	144
Boat of Garten Riverside Walk	● 🚲	2.5 miles	1½ hours	146
Boat of Garten Woodland Walks	●(v) 🚲	1.2 miles (L)	-	148
Loch Garten & Garten Woods	● 🚲	5.5 miles	2½ hours	150
Carrbridge area				
Carrbridge Circuit Trail	● 🚲	3 miles	1½hours	152
Carrbridge Woodland Trails	●(v) 🚲	2.5 miles (L)	-	154
Docharn Woods Walk	◉	5 miles	2½ hours	156
Landmark Adventure Trails	● 🚲	Short Strolls	-	158
Sluggan Bridge Walk	●	2 miles (1)	1 hour	160
The Gurkha Bridge Walk	● 🚲	2 miles	40 minutes	162

Featured Walks at a Glance

● Easy   ● Moderate   ● Challenging   🏛 Good Family Walk - (1) = 1 Way - **V** = Various

WALK	GRADE	DISTANCE	TIME	PAGE
Grantown-on-Spey				
Anagach Woods	● (V) 🏛	5 miles (L)	-	164
General Wade's Military Road	● 🏛	2.5 miles	1½ hours	166
Grantown-on-Spey River Walk	●	7 miles	2½ hours	168
Kylintra Meadows	● (V) 🏛	Short Strolls	-	170
Revach Estate	●● (V) 🏛	5.5 miles (L)	-	172
The Blue Trail Beachen Woods	●	2 miles	1½ hours	174
Viewpoints Walk	●	3 miles	1½ hours	176
Waterfall Walk	●	1.5 miles	1½ hours	178
Nethy Bridge				
Broomhill River Walk	●	3 miles	1½ hours	180
Castle Roy Loop	●	3.5 miles	1¾ hours	182
Lettoch Walk	●	5 miles	2½ hours	184
Nethy Bridge Circuit	●	6.2 miles	2½ hours	186
Nethy Bridge to Boat of Garten	●	5 miles	2 hours	188
Nethy Bridge Woodland Walks	● 🏛	4 miles	1½ hours	190
Riverside & Dell Woods Walk	● 🏛	2 miles	1½ hours	192
Wilderness Trail	● 🏛	1.5 miles	1 hour	194
Glenlivet / Tomintoul & Strathdon				
Glenlivet / Tomintoul				
Braes Heritage Trail	●	4 miles	1½ hours	202
Bochel Circuit	●	6.2 miles	2½ hours	204
Clash Wood	● 🏛	2 miles	1 hour1	206
Drumin Circular & Castle	● 🏛	2 miles	1 hour	208
Geln Brown - Kylnadrochit	●	4 miles	1½ hours	210
Glenconglass to Carn Daimh	●	7.3 miles	3 hours	212
Glenmulliach Nature Trail	● 🏛	3 miles	1½ hour	214
Knock Earth House Walk	●	2.6 miles (1)	1¼ hours	216
Tom Dubh Wood Walk	● 🏛	1.5 miles	45 minutes	218
Tomnavoulin - Carn Daimh	● 🏛	5 miles	2½ hour	220
Strathdon				
Ben Newe Forest Trail	● 🏛	2.2 miles (L)	-	222

WALK	GRADE	DISTANCE	TIME	PAGE
Kincraig & Kingussie				
Kincraig				
Farleitter Crag & Ridge Walk	●	2.2 miles	1½ hours	**230**
Feshiebridge Woodland Walk	● 🌲	3 miles	1 hour	**232**
Kincraig Speyside & Woods	● 🌲	1.2 miles	40 minutes	**234**
River Feshie & Sculpture Trail	● 🌲	1.2 miles	45 minutes	**236**
Loch Insh Interpretative Trail	● 🌲	1 mile	30 minutes	**238**
The Duke of Gordon's Monument	●	2.4 miles	2 hours	**240**
Uath Lochans	● 🌲	1 mile	35 minute	**242**
Uath Lochans to Feshiebridge	●	2.8 mile	1½ hours	**244**
Kingussie				
Birch Woodie	● 🌲	1.2 mile	25 minutes	**246**
Creag Bheag - Loch Gynack	●	3.7 miles	2 hours	**248**
Insh Marshes	● 🌲	2.3 mile	2 hours	**250**
Jubilee Walk / Ruthven Barracks	● 🌲	1.2 miles	20 minutes	**252**
Kingussie Golf Course Walk	●	1.5 miles	1½ hours	**254**
Ruthven Barracks & Glen Tromie	●	6 miles	2¾ hours	**256**
Tom Baraidh Walk	● 🌲	2.5 miles	1½ hours	**258**
West Terrace Circular	●	1.6 miles	1 hour	**260**
Laggan & Newtonmore				
Laggan				
Allt Mhoraich Trail	●	3.4 miles	1¾ hours	**266**
Blackwood & the Pictish Fort	●	5 miles	2¾ hours	**268**
Druim an Aird & Pattack Falls	● 🌲	1.2 miles	1 hour	**270**
Glen Truim Woods & View Point	●	1.9 miles	1 hour	**272**
Gorstean Crag Walk	● 🌲	1 mile	1¼ hours	**274**
Laggan River Spey Walk	● 🌲	1.7 miles	1 hour	**276**
Newtonmore				
Cat of 6 Trails	● 🌲	3 (L)	-	**278**
Highland Folk Museum Tour	● 🌲	1 mile	-	**280**
Loch Imrich Walk	● 🌲	500 metres	20 minutes	**282**
Wildcat Circular Trail	●	6.2 miles	2½ hours	**284**

Angus Glens

The Angus Glens are the lesser-known area of the Cairngorms National Park, and yet this is an area of outstanding beauty with stunning glens and glorious hills that make walking here a joy no matter what type of walking you are into.

There are five glens and all are easy to reach via towns like Aboyne and Blairgowrie, however, unlike the other regions in the park, there are no large villages or towns in the glens, but rather there is a series of small hamlets offering basic local services to walkers all year round.

The glens have a collection of long hill walks for the more experienced walker linking the area with Braemar and Ballater, and short family walks through forest where rare animals thrive, around castles and alongside lochs and rivers.

Many of the walks have long historical links, namely The Queen's Well in Glen Mark and Jock's Road in Glen Doll, which neighbours the Corrie Fee Nature Reserve which in turn is one of the most important reserves in the UK, and as well as being an area where rare alpine plants exist, the corrie also supports rare birds such as golden eagles and crossbills.

Glendoll Forest Walk (see page 22)

Invermark to the Queen's Well Walk (see page 26)

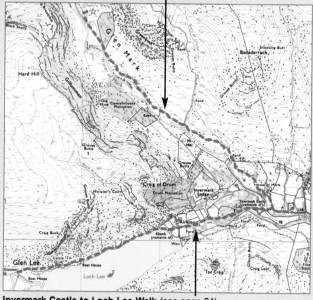

Invermark Castle to Loch Lee Walk (see page 24)

Loch Brandy Walk (see page 28)

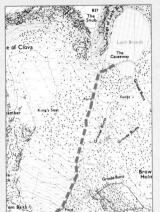

South Esk Loop (see page 30)

South Esk River Walk (see page 32)

The Dounalt Walk (see page 34)

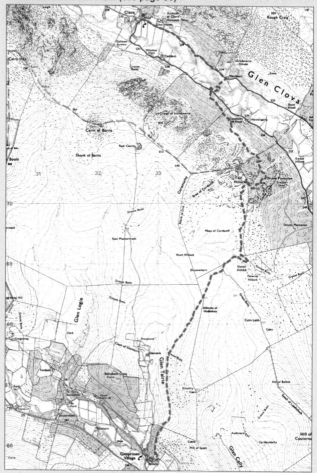

Walk up to Corrie Fee Nature Reserve (see page 38)

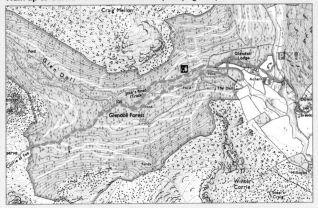

White Water Trail Walk (see page 40)

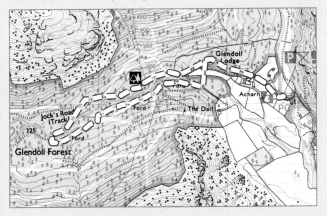

Glendoll Forest Walk

<u>Glen Clova - Glen Doll</u>   see walk diagram on map page 18

Walk Data

Orientation
Circuit route

Length
3 miles (5 km)

Grade
● Easy

Time
1½ hours

Height Gain
110m (360ft)

Hills & Steeps
Steep hill section

Terrain
Surfaced & natural

Route Marks
▶ Red marker

Wheelchairs
No access

Access for Prams
Not suitable

Key Features

Wood & water trail with varied wildlife

Good View points

White Water

Noise Indicator

Quiet walk with bird, wind and water noise.

Walk starts from the Glen Doll Car Park

The Dell Woods have a number of walks, of which some are a doddle and some are not, and while this is a relatively no-nonsense and simple walk, it's still a long haul up a hill. But fear not - the route is not via a rough or uneven trail but up a wide, flat, hard path.

Join the walk from the Glen Doll car park by turning right along the road which runs to the west of the car park and walk past the small collection of farm houses. Just ahead you will see four marker posts with route names on them. Select the Doll Walk and, as directed, turn left and walk over the bridge to follow the red marker posts.

The walk soon heads uphill and becomes steepest as it turns back on itself a couple of times, before straightening out into a clearing where a lot of forestry work has taken place, and while the first part of this walk is up a decent hill, what you do not need to do is to waste money on expensive boots or gizmos such as daft collapsible ski poles (what numpty came up with these "must-have" accessories for walkers?).

However, this is a great walk for those who don't fancy the longer routes up to the Corrie Fee Nature reserve or the Dounalt trail, which both travel through Doll Woods. Eventually the route meets up with the Burn of Kilbo, which you follow back down to meet up with the route known as the White Water trail, way-marked with the white-banded posts.

The woods are home to lots of varying wildlife and plant species, and if you keep yours eyes peeled you may well see deer, red squirrels and all manner of birds - sometimes including the elusive Scottish crossbill.

 It's a good walk with a dog, with no farm animals to worry about after the fields at the start

Location: Glen Clova is reached off the B955 to Dykehead where you take the right fork signposted to Clova at which you drive for 3 miles to the road end at the Glen Doll pay and display car park.

Crossbill

Extras

 There is a pay and display car park at the base of Glen Doll Forest costing from around £1.50.

 Male and female toilets are provided next to the car park.

Nearest:
Accommodation - The Glen Clova Hotel is located 3 miles back down the glen in the hamlet of Clova. tel. (01575) 550350
Food - Glen Clova Hotel
Fuel Station - at Kirriemuir, 14.5 miles back down the glen.

Invermark Castle - Loch Lee

Glen Esk - Glen Lee see walk diagram on map page 18

Walk Data

Orientation
Point to Point

Length *(return)*
4.4 miles (7km)

Grade
● Easy

Time *(return)*
2 hours

Height Gain
Minimal

Hills & Steeps
Flat

Terrain
Surfaced & natural

Route Marks
No way markers

Wheelchairs
Passable

Access for Prams
Passable

Key Features

Water trail with varied wildlife

Good View points

Castle

Loch Lee

Noise Indicator

Quiet spot with only natural sounds.

Walk starts from the Invermark Car Park

Invermark Castle and Loch Lee are located in a remote area at the head of Glen Esk, 4 miles on from the small village of Tarfside.

The walk starts from the ruins of Invermark Castle, which dates back to 1526. The place was built by the Lindsay family to the typical keep design and it has had a long and colourful history. Locals from Invermark would shelter here when raiders descended on the glen to steal cattle and pillage the villagers' goods. Over the centuries numerous dignitaries have sought to escape retribution from rivals and government troops. Lord Balnamoon once hid here after Culloden, as did David Lindsay who in 1607 killed Lord Spynie in Edinburgh after a long-standing quarrel.

Today the castle is boarded up and access is not possible on the grounds of safety.

The walk from the car park takes you past two ruins, that of the castle and an old church, and despite being a remote location it's a very simple trail along a wide, flat vehicle track which runs along the loch's northern shore line.

There is nothing adventurous about it, no obstacles to surmount or steep hills to climb. The walk gently travels along a path with great views. It can end at the loch at the small bridge, where you could turn round and return as you came, while those feeling more energetic and adventurous can take in the Falls of Unich, another 4.5 miles on, along a recognised track. You can continue further and take in the Falls of Damff, but both these extensions add a fair amount of extra mileage and take the walk from an easy trail to a long, testing hill climb.

 There are no worries regarding the dog, but livestock may be in some fields near the start of the walk, so keep the dog on a lead until you reach the loch.

Location: Glen Esk can be reached on the B966 which is 15 miles from Invermark along the glen via Tarfside.

Stoat

Extras

 Free parking is available at Invermark just yards from Invermark Castle.

 There are public toilets available in Tarfside, which is 4 miles from Invermark.

Nearest:
Accommodation - B&B's, hotels and guests houses etc are all available in town of Edzell, some 16 miles back down the glen.
Food - There is a cafe/restaurant at the Retreat Museum 5 miles back down the glen.
Fuel Station - Edzell, 16 miles away

25

Invermark to the Queen's Well

see walk diagram on map page 18

Walk Data

Walk starts from the Invermark Car Park

Orientation
Point to Point

Length *(Return)*
5 miles (8km)

Grade
● Moderate

Time *(return)*
3 hours

Height Gain
60m (197ft)

Hills & Steeps
Long gradent

Terrain
Hard stoned path

Route Marks
None

Wheelchairs
No access

Access for Prams
Not suitable

Key Features

Moorland trail with varied wildlife

Good View points

Historic Monument

Water of Mark

Noise Indicator

The only noise is the sound of the wind.

Glen Esk forms part of the Grampian mountain range and is the most easterly of the Angus Glens.

The walk up to the Queen's Well is a rough hill trek crossing a stretch of barren moorland, which on a windy day will have you heading for cover. The walk forms part a challenging and far longer high hill climb which takes you up to Mount Keen, the most easterly of the Munros, which rises to a summit of 940m. From Glen Esk the route over Mount Keen would take you to either Ballater or Glen Tannar in the north.

However, the route to the well is not over-testing or dramatic and provided you are reasonably fit, you should have no problems tackling this rough heather clad moorland trail which rewards its visitors with stunning panoramic views.

From the Invermark car park you set off down the road and after a few yards you turn right at the sign for the Queen's Well and Invermark House. In front of the house and the brick wall, you turn left and walk down the track passing through a gate and into a rough patch of land with sheep. The path you join is studded with stones and rocks and is rough in places, but easily negotiated. After walking up the path for 5 minutes you will come to an old metal gate, which you pass through en route to the monument two and half miles on.

Meadow Pipit

The Queen's Well is a crown-shaped stone construction commemorating a visit by Queen Victoria and Prince Albert in 1861 after they travelled over from Balmoral Castle to picnic here.

Look out for red deer, mountain hares and various moorland birds. Adders can also be found in these parts.

Extras

 Free parking is available at Invermark just yards from Invermark Castle.

 There are public toilets available in Tarfside, which is 4 miles from Invermark.

 Nearest:
Accommodation - B&B's, hotels and guests houses etc are all available in town of Edzell, some 16 miles back down the glen.
Food - There is a cafe/restaurant at the Retreat Museum 5 miles back down the glen
Fuel Station - Edzell, 16 miles away.

Sheep may be in the field at the start but the rest of the walk is fine with a dog off the lead.

Location: Glen Esk can be reached on the B966 which is 15 miles from Invermark along the glen via Tarfside.

Loch Brandy Walk

Glen Clova see walk diagram on map page 19

Walk Data

Orientation
Point to Point

Length (return)
3 miles (4.8 km)

Grade
● Challenging

Time (return)
2 hours

Height Gain
410m (1345ft)

Hills & Steeps
Very steep

Walk starts behind Clova Hotel

Terrain
Surfaced & natural

Route Marks
No markings

Wheelchairs
No access

Access for Prams
Not suitable

Key Features

Moorland trail with varied wildlife

Good View points

Loch Brandy

Noise Indicator

Very quiet walk with only wind noise.

Loch Brandy is a high corrie loch, easily reached via a well-defined track - but it's steep and will test you if you were out on the sauce the night before!

By the time you get to the loch any hangover will have gone: this is brisk hill walk up a moorland path that's unforgiving. But don't be put off, it's not a trek just for the serious walkers with GPS navigation and oxygen masks, unless you want to do the full ridge and two lochs circuit via Loch Wharral.

It's uphill all the way to the loch and back but the fine hard track is easy to follow, even if it isn't way-marked. The walk starts from a path through a small gate behind the Clova Hotel. Here you walk through a few trees and over a small wooden bridge before reaching a round metal swing gate. As soon as you pass through the gate you join a gritted track which immediately heads uphill, getting steeper as it ascends. The path is easy-going though, and there are no major surprises or any tricky sections.

Hen Harrier

The path continues in a northerly direction and providing it's a good clear day, the views are stunning. However, should you get caught in a bad weather there is no shelter and if wind is blowing you'll certainly know all about it. After walking for 40 minutes you will reach the loch, which sits at the base of a hill. There is path up to and around the loch via The Snub, but unless you are an experienced hill walker, stick to the shorter walk and, after chilling out at the loch-side, simply retrace your steps back down to the start.

The eastern sections of the Cairngorms have the largest breeding concentrations of hen harriers, which like heather moorlands, so keep an eye out for them.

Extras

There is a free parking at the Milton of Glen Clova car park, which is at the front of Clova Hotel just after the bend and bridge crossing .

The only restriction is the short stretch up to the metal gate, where dogs should be kept on a lead.

Male and female toilets are provided next to the car park.

Nearest:
Accommodation - The Glen Clova Hotel is located at the start of the walk. tel: (01575) 550350
Food - Glen Clova Hotel
Fuel Station - at Kirriemuir, 10.5 miles back down the glen.

Location: Clova is reached off the B955 via Dykehead and the walks starts from behind the Clova hotel.

South Esk Loop & Trout Loch Walk

see walk diagram on map page 19

Walk Data

Orientation
Circuit route

Length
2.5 miles (4 km)

Grade
● Easy

Time
1 hour

Height Gain
Minimal

Hills & Steeps
Flat walk

Terrain
Soft earth & road

Route Marks
None

Wheelchairs
No access

Access for Prams
Not suitable

Key Features

Wood & water trail with varied wildlife

Good View points

River South Esk

Noise Indicator

Natural sounds and the odd car passing.

Walk starts from opposite Clova Hotel

The South Esk Loop and Trout Loch Walk is a bit of a no-brainer and although the local information board in the Milton Car Park has these two marked down as two separate walks, in reality they're almost non-existent and require you, basically, to make it up as you go.

The walks are based around or close to the South Esk, a long river flowing the entire length of Glen Clova, rising in the Grampian Mountains and eventually flowing into the North Sea at the Montrose Basin. The river is very popular with anglers hoping for salmon and trout.

The loop walk is somewhat confusing, since it has no clearly discernible path, but at the same time it's a very easy, low-level one around a small section of the river. However, there is neither a proper start point nor a full way-marked track to follow.

The Esk loop travels around the river and this is the easiest way to go: from opposite the car park, next to the Glen Clova Hotel, you will see an old wooden fence, where you can simply cross into the field and take the short walk to the river's edge, where you turn left and follow the water for a mile until you come to a small bridge. After crossing, either turn right and follow the river back to the start along the opposite bank, or you can head up to the road following a marker post of another walk, turning right to walk back along the road to the start point in Clova. Note that the land through the fields to the river can be wet and muddy and there may well be livestock. There is also an electric fence at the river's edge.

The Trout Loch Walk is along a dedicated path in front of the hotel car park. You walk for nearly a mile until you come to the small lochan on your left. Fishing permits are available at Glen Clova Hotel.

 Both walks are either in fields with livestock or along a road, so keep the dog on the lead.

Location: Clova is reached off the B955 via Dykehead and the walk starts from behind the Clova hotel.

What 'ewe' looking at?

Extras

 There is free parking at the Milton of Glen Clova car park, which is at the front of Clova Hotel just after the bend and bridge crossing .

 Male and female toilets are provided next to the car park.

Nearest:
Accommodation - The Glen Clova Hotel is located at the start of the walk. tel: (01575) 550350
Food - Glen Clova Hotel
Fuel Station - at Kirriemuir, 10.5 miles back down the glen.

31

South Esk River Walk

Glen Clova - Glen Doll   see walk diagram on map page 19

Walk Data

Orientation
Circuit route

Length
2 miles (3.2 km)

Grade
● Easy

Time
1 hour

Height Gain
Minimal

Hills & Steeps
Gental low rise

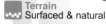
Terrain
Surfaced & natural

Route Marks
▶ Yellow banding

Wheelchairs
No access

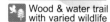
Access for Prams
Passable

Key Features

🌲 Wood & water trail with varied wildlife

📷 Good View points

🏊 River South Esk

Noise Indicator

🔊 The only sounds are wildlife and natural.

Walk starts from the Glen Doll Car Park

The walk around the upper section of the River South Esk is the easiest of all the way-marked trails in the Glen Doll Forest, and it's a walk that the whole family, including toddlers, can do with ease. If you have a good off-road pram most of the walk is easy to negotiate, but there are a few spots towards the end of the walk, down the left side of the river as you face uphill, where the path is a bit narrow and becomes a little bumpy.

The walk takes you to the upper parts of Glen Clova, which has been naturally sculpted over many thousands of years from the Ice Age, leaving corries, cliffs, moraines and waterways. These days parts of the River Esk have become a conservation area with a particular interest in protecting freshwater mussels, which are increasingly rare and a threatened species protected under Scottish law.

The walk starts from the car park and by following the yellow marker post at the entrance to the site, you walk across a bridge and immediately turn left and walk up the eastern side of the river. The first part of the walk is along a wide and hard-based vehicle track and begins through a clearing before travelling through a pinewood.

Around the halfway mark you come up against a fence and a gate. Turn left as directed by the marker and walk down a clearing which reveals a wooden bridge crossing the river. There is also a pretty wooden bench to chill out on before heading across the bridge and walking back down to the beginning. For the second leg of the walk, the track becomes softer and narrow in parts, but it never gets hard or tricky and you eventually arrive back at a small grass area, with picnic tables next to the car park.

 It's a good walk with a dog - no livestock to worry about.

Location: Glen Clova is reached off the B955 to Dykehead where you take the right fork signposted to Clova at which you drive for 3 miles to the road end at the Glen Doll pay and display car park.

Dipper

Extras

 There is a pay and display car park at the base of Glen Doll Forest costing from around £1.50.

 Male and female toilets are provided next to the car park.

 Nearest:
Accommodation - The Glen Clova Hotel is located 3 miles back down the glen in the hamlet of Clova. tel, (01575) 550350
Food - Glen Clova Hotel
Fuel Station - at Kirriemuir, 14.5 miles back down the glen.

The Dounalt Walk

Glen Clova - Glen Doll

see walk diagram on map page 19

Walk Data

Orientation
Circuit rote

Length
5 miles (8 km)

Grade
● Moderate

Time
2½ hours

Height Gain
170m (558ft)

Hills & Steeps
Long hill

Terrain
Surfaced & natural

Route Marks
▶ Blue marlers

Wheelchairs
No access

Access for Prams
Not suitable

Key Features

Wood & water trail with varied wildlife

Good View points

White Water

Noise Indicator

Birds singing in the trees and walkers.

Walk starts from the Glen Doll Car Park

The Dounalt Walk joins up with the famous Jock's Road, the first Scottish Right of Way, and links Glen Clova with Braemar via Glen Callater, some 14 miles across a high mountain pass which should only be walked by well-equipped, experienced walkers - it's a wild place!

But the walk known as the Dounalt is a forest one, through the upper section of the Glen Doll Forest and can be tackled by anyone prepared to trek two and a half miles up hill and then two and half miles1/2 down again along a well-worn but decent path.

The route travels up hill following the blue marker posts tracing White Water burn as it goes. Initially the trek takes in a simple, wide vehicle track, which attracts lots of walkers (sometimes it feels a bit like Princes Street on a Saturday morning).

From the car park you head right up the farm track and after half a mile you come to a fork in the road where there is a memorial and a sign for Jock's Road. Turn right and join the narrow track which leads into a thick, dark wood. The route continues to gain height as it weaves its way along with the water running down to your left. Eventually you will come to the edge of the forest, as clearly designated by a tall deer fence - this is the halfway point and you simply cross the small footbridge to your left down a short path and return down into the forest along the trail opposite the White Water.

The forest here is simply bursting with wildlife and the air is full of birdsong. Red squirrels go about their business of collecting nuts while herons can be seen gliding through the more open sections.

The walk is good for the dog with no farm animals to worry about apart from any which might be in the field right at the start.

Location: Glen Clova is reached off the B955 to Dykehead where you take the right fork signposted to Clova at which you drive for 3 miles to the roads end at the Glen Doll pay and display car park.

Extras

There is a pay and display car park at the base of Glen Doll Forest costing from around £1.50.

Male and female toilets are provided next to the car park.

Nearest:
Accommodation - The Glen Clova Hotel is located 3 miles back down the glen in the hamlet of Clova. tel, (01575) 550350
Food - Glen Clova Hotel
Fuel Station - at Kirriemuir, 14.5 miles back down the glen.

The Minister's Path

Glen Clova - Glen Prosen

see walk diagram on map page 20

Walk Data

Orientation
Point to Point

Length *(one way)*
6 miles (9.7 km)

Grade
● Challenging

Time *(one way)*
3 hours

Height Gain
220m (722ft)

Hills & Steeps
Very hilly

Terrain
Vehicle tracks

Route Marks
▶ Purple arrow

Wheelchairs
No access

Access for Prams
Not suitable

Key Features

Wood & moorland
with varied wildlife

Good View points

River South Esk

Noise Indicator

Quiet walk with only
wind rush as you go.

Walk starts from opposite Clova Hotel

This walk is so called because it was the route used by the local minister in Clova who would travel on horse to reach Glen Prosen on a Sunday in order to practise his trade, sing out of tune and fill up his coffers with money donated by the poor.

The route is not for those who don't like long hill walks, and note this is a point-to-point walk, so you will either have to walk back the way you came to reach your vehicle, or you will have to arrange a pick-up in Glen Prosen Village at the walk's end.

You have two options as far as the end point is concerned: Either do the shorter walk to Prosen Village or the much longer alternative down to the Airlie Memorial Tower, which is visible for miles and was built in 1901 in honour of David Ogilvy, the 9th Earl of Airlie who was killed during the Boer War.

Start the walk from the car park in front of the Glen Clova Hotel and head south along the minor road passing the trout loch on your left. A mile on you will come to a white house called Inchdownie - opposite it, you walk into a field and head for the river. You will soon see a wooden bridge. Cross it and follow the purple marker arrows from this point on. About 100 meters up the path, having turned left along a fence, you come to a road. Cross over and turn left until you come to a high stile crossing into a clearing. Climb over here and walk along the vehicle track following the purple arrows as you go. The route takes you up hill paths, which at times can be very faint, so it's highly recommended that you study a map and plot the route beforehand to avoid getting lost, especially if you want to walk down to the Airlie Memorial tower. See OS Explorer map 3880

Grey Partridge

 Some farm animals around the bridge, but after that the route is a good run for dogs.

Location: Clova is reached off the B955 via Dykehead and the walk starts from behind the Clova hotel. Local transport is very limited, however there is a postbus service that travels to and from Kirriemuir.

Extras

 There is free parking at the Milton of Glen Clova car park, which is at the front of Clova Hotel just after the bend and bridge crossing .

 Male and female toilets are provided next to the car park.

Nearest:
Accommodation - The Glen Clova Hotel is located at the start of the walk. tel: (01575) 550350
Food - Glen Clova Hotel
Fuel Station - at Kirriemuir, 10.5 miles back down the glen.

Walk up to Corrie Fee Nature Reserve

Glen Clova - Glen Doll

see walk diagram on map page 21

Walk Data

Orientation
Point to Point

Length *(return)*
4 miles (6.5 km)

Grade
● Easy

Time *(return)*
2 hours

Height Gain
180m (590ft)

Hills & Steeps
Long high hill

Terrain
Hard surfaced path

Route Marks
▶ Green marking

Wheelchairs
No access

Access for Prams
Not suitable

Key Features

Wood & water trail
with varied wildlife

Good View points

Whie Water

Noise Indicator

Quiet walk with bird, wind and water noise.

Walk starts from the Glen Doll Car Park

There has long been a recognised trail up Corrie Fee, but the route was in great need of improvement to make it easier and more accessible, and thanks to a substantial amount of money being spent and ten months hard work, that's exactly what has happened.

The walk starts from the car park and winds its way up through the Glen Doll forest to Corrie Fee, which is a spectacular area of rock faces, cliffs, corries and waterfalls. From the car park you follow the green marker post heading along a wide, hard and well-maintained track. The path travels along the White Water burn en-route through pine trees. It's a gentle walk and not too testing, and although it's uphill all the way, it's not steep and there are no obstacles to climb. The walk back down is via the same path to the car park, or by following the White Water trail, which has white marker posts.

As you near the top you will come to a small stone bridge, here you cross over and head up the short stepped path to a gate and fence. This is the entrance to the Corrie Fee Nature Reserve, which is one of the most important areas in the UK for rare alpine plants, such as yellow oxytropis, an alpine thistle which grows on ledges, and purple saxifrage thriving in high mountain regions with cold climates.

Golden Eagle

Corrie Fee is also an important area for wildlife and there is a European conservation project in place dedicated to looking after golden eagles - if you're lucky you just might see one soaring high over the hills in search of prey.

The hut in the car park has details of the local area. There are also toilets and next to the river is a picnic site with great views.

 Except for the fields around the very start the walk is a good one with a dog, with no farm animals to worry about.

Location: Glen Clova is reached off the B955 to Dykehead where you take the right fork signposted to Clova at which you drive for 3 miles to the road end at the Glen Doll pay and display car park.

Extras

 There is a pay and display car park at the base of Glen Doll Forest costing from around £1.50.

 Male and female toilets are provided next to the car park.

Nearest:
Accommodation - The Glen Clova Hotel is located 3 miles back down the glen in the hamlet of Clova.
tel, (01575) 550350
Food - Glen Clova Hotel
Fuel Station - at Kirriemuir, 14.5 miles back down the glen.

Golden Eagle - Carl Mckie

White Water Trail

Glen Clova - Glen Doll   see walk diagram on map page 21

Walk Data

 Orientation
Circuit route

 Length
2.5 miles (4 km)

 Grade
● Easy

 Time
1½ hours

 Height Gain
80m (262ft)

 Hills & Steeps
Easy hill

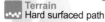 **Terrain**
Hard surfaced path

 **Route Marks**
▶ White markers

 Wheelchairs
No access

Access for Prams
Passable

Key Features

🐿 Wood & water trail
with varied wildlife

📷 Good View points

🌊 White Water

Noise Indicator

👂 Quiet walk with bird,
wind and water noise.

Walk starts from the Glen Doll Car Park

This is a sheltered circular walk - through a section of pine trees and along a water stretch - but note: the notice board at the car park shows the walk in black, but in fact you follow the marker posts with a white ring round them.

The walk is easy, beginning from the car park and turning left along the farm road. A few hundred meters past the farm buildings on the right, you will come to a junction with a series or waymarker posts. At this point, take the track to the left as directed by the marker post and follow the hard path, alongside the waters on your right. Keep on the path, passing the turn-off for Jock's Road on your right, and after about 25 minutes you will come to a another junction just past a short bridge. At the junction, look out for the round marker post with a white band on your left, next to a small track leading into the trees. Follow this path back down to the car park though the woods, pass-

40

ing through a tunnel of overhead branches and crossing a small wooden bridge as you go. Eventually you come to yet another junction, where you turn left and head back down the outward farm road.

Water Vole

There are no great surprises or any trouble spots along what is a great family walk. Children who like to play hide and seek have plenty of trees to hide behind, and lots of nature to discover.

The water around the woods used to be home to water voles, but with the emergence of American mink in the area they've been virtually wiped out. Conservation efforts are now in place to keep the mink at bay, which is helping to bring the voles back.

The walk is a good one with a dog, with no farm animals to worry about after the fields at the very start.

Location: Glen Clova is reached off the B955 to Dykehead where you take the right fork signposted to Clova at which you drive for 3 miles to the road end at the Glen Doll pay and display car park.

Extras

There is a pay and display car park at the base of Glen Doll Forest costing from around £1.50.

Male and female toilets are provided next to the car park.

Nearest:
Accommodation - The Glen Clova Hotel is located 3 miles back down the glen in the hamlet of Clova.
tel, (01575) 550350
Food - Glen Clova Hotel
Fuel Station - at Kirriemuir, 14.5 miles back down the glen.

Aviemore & Glenmore

The Aviemore and Glenmore areas are probably the most visited places for walkers in the whole of the Cairngorms National Park area with dozens of walks and trails for all abilities, and it's easy to see why, with a choice from snowcapped mountain walks to simple fun trails around nature reserves and lochans.

Around Aviemore itself, there are a couple of interesting walks, which include the marked trails in the Craigellachie Nature Reserve known for its population of Peregrine Falcons who nest high on the crags. However, it's on the outskirts of the village where you will find some walking gems on the Rothiemurchus Estate or on the lands managed by the Forestry Commision at Glenmore.

Rothiemurchus is a large highland estate where you will find lots of stunning walks. The estate offers many well laid out and way marked trails with an easy to follow map. There arealso ranger walking services available.

Glenmore Forest is a notable pine forest and here you can enjoy numerous walks that could take you years if you wanted to walk every known path. However, you don't need a decade to do the easy family walks located near or around the popular and scenic Loch Morlich.

www.cairngormslivingwalks.com

Allt Mor All Abilities Trail (see page 50)

Aviemore Orbital path (see page 54)

Allt Mor Trail up to the Cairngorms (see page 52)

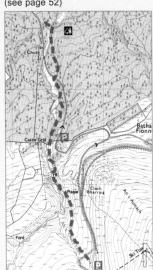

Aviemore Speyside Golf Walk (see page 56)

Aviemore to Boat of Garten (see page 58)

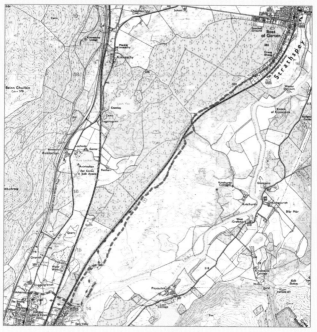

Corie Cas Lower Loop Walk
(see page 60)

Coylumbridge to the Iron Bridge
(see page 62)

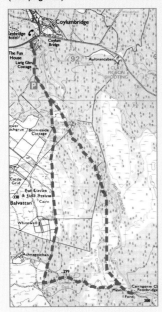

Glenmore Forest Trail
(see page 66)

Lily Loch Walk
(see page 68)

Craigellachie Nature Reserve
(see page 64)

For full size maps: www.cairngormslivingwalks.com

Loch an Eilein Circular Trail (see page 70)

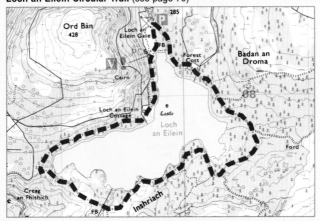

Loch Morlich Circular (see page 72)

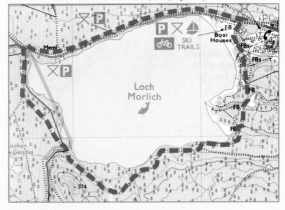

Maps - by permission of Ordnance Survey
CrownCopyright Licence N0 100048399

Loch nan Carriagean Stone Circle
(see page 74)

Loch Vaa
(see page 78)

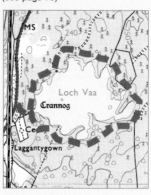

Lochan nan Nathrach Trail (see page 76)

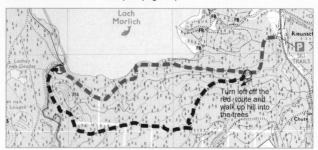

Turn left off the red route and walk up hill into the trees

Ryvoan & Green Loch Trex (see page 80)

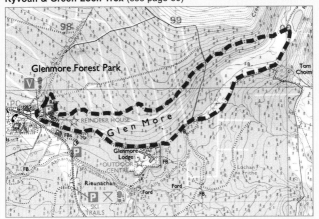

The Queen's Forest Walk (see page 82)

The Woodland Trail
(see page 84)

Allt Mor All Abilities Trail

Walk Data

Orientation
Circuit route

Length
400m

Grade
● Easy

Time
20 minutes

Height Gain
Minimal

Hills & Steeps
Flat walk

Terrain
Surfaced trail

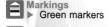
Markings
► Green markers

Wheelchairs
Full access

Access for Prams
Full access

Key Features

Wood & water trail with varied wildlife

Good View point

Picnic site

Information posts

Noise Indicator

Forest sounds plus the odd vehicle noise.

Start the walk from the Allt Mor Car Park.

Located east of Aviemore at the foothills of the Cairngorms, this is a first class family walk for all ages and all abilities, which includes a special section for the disabled.

Set in a stunning location next to the Allt Mor fast flowing burn with a pine forest and the Cairngorm Mountains forming a majestic back drop, this is a walk to while away half an hour on Sunday afternoon (any afternoon in fact) where kids can learn all about the forest from the information on the pop up interpretation panels which line the top end of the trail close the shore line of the Allt Mor burn.

The walk starts from the Allt Mor car park, which is reached 1/4 a mile past the Glenmore Visitor Centre on the left of the road as you head up the Cairngom mountain road. Follow the green marker post, which at times shares the post with a yellow marker for another walk.

The car park is made up of small bays, so look out for the markers behind the bays that sit closest to the waterside. Walking in an anti-clock wise direction simply follow the green waymarkers. The track is surfaced and easy to walk on, although there are a couple of bumpy bits which wheelchair users may notice, and should it be raining, then a wheelchair or pram could find it a bit hard going as the path could be rather soft.

Caterpillar

Along the top end of the route, you will find some posts with descriptions about the trees, the plants and the wildlife living in the forest. Look out for juniper, which is a hardy shrub with green berries. Juniper grows around pine trees like the ones that grow here. You will able to read all about Scots pine as well as find out about what herbs you can discover or what insects to look out for, such as wood ants and caterpillars.

Extras

 Parking is available at the start of the walk 1/4 of a mile past the Glenmore Visitor Centre.

 Nearest toilets are Glenmore Visitor Centre 1/4 of a mile along the road.

 Nearest:
Accommodation - Camp site and Youth Hostel near the start.
visit - www.visitaviemore.com
Food - Glenmore Visitor Centre.
Fuel Station - Aviemore, 6 miles.

 Contact for further details:
Glenmore Visitor Centre
www.forestry.gov.uk
tel (01479) 861 220

The Forestry Commission ask you to keep dogs on the lead at all times as this is an area with ground nesting birds.

Location: The Allt Mor Car Park is located next to the Cairngorm snow gates just past the Glenmore visitor centre.

Allt Mor Trail up to the Cairngorms

Aviemore - Glenmore   see walk diagram on map page 44

Walk Data

Orientation
Point to Point

Length *(one way)*
3½ miles (5.6km)

Grade
● Moderate

Time *(one way)*
2 hours

Height Gain
300m (984ft)

Hills & Steeps
Long hill

Terrain
Surfaced path

Markings
🌿 Tree disc

Wheelchairs
No access

Access for Prams
Not suitable

Key Features

🌲 Wood & water trail
with varied wildlife

📷 Good View points

🌊 Allt Mor Burn

Noise Indicator

🔊 The main sound is
water rushing down.

Start the walk from the Allt Mor Car Park.

The trail up to the Cairngorms from the Allt Mor car park in the Glenmore forest is an excellent point-to-point walk that starts out in a pine forest and finishes up on the Cairngorms with views that stretch for miles on a clear day.

It's not a walk for everyone as it involves a trek with a height gain of almost 1000 feet. That said, the trail is never over testing and the path is so easy to walk along that you hardly notice the incline. A point to note is that the walk is a point to point walk, which will take about 2 hours one way. However, you can get a local bus back down from the Day Lodge car park, which is where the walk ends, to pick up your vehicle.

Start the walk from the top end of the Alt Mor car park and follow the marker post with the tree discs. To find the route you look out for the car park sign showing way out, from this

Get a large map of this walk at - www.cairngormslivingwalks.com

point look to your left and you will just see a track leading to a thin long wooden bridge that spans the Allt Mor burn. Cross the bridge and turn sharp right and begin the walk, which starts out through the trees alongside the water. After a short while the path travels along a wooden surface that winds through an opening and leads to the sur-faced path again before reaching the main road that travels up to the Cairngorms at the road end. Unfortunately, some drivers devoid of brain cells are known for hurtling down this road at speed, so take great care and cross over the road and pick the path again, which leads along to some wooden foot bridges within a wooded stretch and along the banks of the burn, which you follow for the length of the walk. After a while the path leaves the tree-lined section and enters an open area of hillside moorland, which you follow up to the bottom level car park.

 The Forestry Commission ask you to keep dogs on the lead at all times as this is an area with ground nesting birds.

Location: The Allt Mor Car Park is located next to the Cairngorm snow gates just past the Glenmore visitor centre.

Reindeer

Extras

 Free parking is available at the Allt Mor car park, but remember this is a point-to-point walk. However, there is public transport available at the Day Lodge, which is where the walk ends. Buses travel back down past the start point car park.

Toilets are available at the Day Lodge near the walk's end point.

Nearest: *(from the walk's end)*
Accommodation - At Glenmore, 2 miles down the mountain road. A much wider selection is available back in Aviemore 10 miles away.
visit - www.visitaviemore.com
Food - At the Day Lodge.
Fuel Station - Aviemore, 10 miles.

53

Aviemore Orbital Path

Walk Data

Orientation
Circuit route

Length
2 miles (3kms)

Grade
● Easy

Time
1 hour

Height Gain
Minimal

Hills & Steeps
Small hill

Walk starts opposite the Spar Shop

Terrain
Dirt paths & tarmac

Markings
Local signs

Wheelchairs
No access

Access for Prams
Not suitable

Key Features

Woodland trail
with varied wildlife

Heather

Birch Trees

Noise Indicator

Loud road noise
from the nearby A9.

The Aviemore Orbital Path is a simple stroll which takes you through part of the village centre and around one side of the perimeter.

A good starting point is opposite the Spar shop along the main road. Here you will pick up a marker post directing you to head west along the path through some trees between the houses. The path takes you past the primary school, and after crossing the Aviemore Burn it leads into Milton Wood's mature Scots Pines which are home to many nesting birds and red squirrels. Various plants and mosses also thrive in these woods.

As you progress, you may encounter a few uneven path features where the odd tree route pokes through or the path becomes a bit loose, but on the whole this is a good track and it's only when there has been a downpour that things get messy.

Once you leave the woods at the northern end of the village, the path travels behind some houses towards Achantoul with a gradual incline. Along this section there are outstanding views across the Cairngorms and on a clear day you can see for miles. Eventually the track turns right and drops down to connect up with the Speyside Way on the other side of the B9152 road at the corner of the Morrison's housing estate (very ugly indeed).

©Great Tit

After crossing the main road, you turn right and take the hard path back into Aviemore. At this point the walk becomes rather feature-less, unless you're into drab look-ing houses, ending at the Spar.

Aviemore Orbital Path

One thing that does stand out about this walk is that it's not a quiet one, and throughout the trail you will hear the noise of vehicles travelling along the A9 (even the rabbits wear ear muffs here).

 Keep dogs on the lead as the A9 is a fast and dangerous road, and it's not securely fenced off from the walk.

Location: The Spar shop is locat-ed in the centre of Aviemore, on the right as you head north towards Inverness.

Extras

 You are advised to park at one of the main public car parks in the centre of Aviemore.

 The nearest public toilets are located in the village centre near the Police station.

 Nearest:
Accommodation - Lots in Aviemore. visit - www.visitaviemore.com
Food - All around Aviemore.
Fuel Station - From the Spar, about 1/2 a mile along Grampian road.

i **Contact for further details:**
Aviemore Tourist Office
0845 2255 121

Aviemore Speyside Golf Walk

Walk Data

Orientation
Circuit route

Length
4.5 miles (7.2kms)

Grade
● Easy

Time
2 hours

Height Gain
Minimal

Hills & Steeps
A few small hills

Terrain
Natural track

Markings
Golf signs

Wheelchairs
Not access

Access for Prams
Not suitable

Key Features

Wood & river trail with varied wildlife

Good View points

Golf Course

Riverside

Noise Indicator

Trains, golfers and some bird songs.

Walk starts from Dalfaber Country Club

Start the walk from the Dalfaber Golf and Country Club car park by heading right along the main road towards the wooden chalets. After a few hundred meters you will see a sign stating 'golf vehicles only': from here turn left into the field and walk down to the river following the fence that separates the two golf courses. At the end of the field you will come to an open gate, here you simply pick up a track and continue going straight ahead until you reach the river's edge. When you reach the river, turn left and follow the path north.

You follow the river for 15 minutes until you reach the 18th tee: just past here you cross a bridge, which takes you to a fork in the track, where you follow the riverside walk sign up a small hill and carry on along the well-defined track. When you reach the 4th tee section, the track moves away from the riverside and heads uphill into a clearing. At the top you will find yourself on the golf course, which you walk round passing a small lochan on the right until you come to a stile crossing the fence close to the 10th tee. Cross the fence and walk down the vehicle track through a heather field until you meet up with the Speyside way. At the fork, turn left and take the path back into Dalfaber, keeping left and following the golf course. When you reach the 18th tee, walk round the outside passing the 1st hole and eventually you will reach a gate with a path that leads straight back to the Country Club car park.

In the woods of Dalfaber lives a shy family of roe deer, and if you keep quiet you may well spot them.

This is a quiet walk, and apart from the odd golfer clad in an ill-fitting pink jumper and moaning about their latest drive, the only sounds you will hear should be the rush of the water, bird song and occasionally the steam train's whistle.

 As this walk is alongside a golf course, keep dogs on the lead at all times (golfers do moan!).

Location: Dalfaber is at the north end of Aviemore off Grampian road 500 metres over the railway line.

Yellowhammer

Extras

 Free parking is available at the Dalfaber Golf and Country Club.

The nearest toilets are in the Dalfaber Golf and Country Club (patrons only). Public toilets are located in the village centre.

 Nearest:
Accommodation - Lots in Aviemore. visit - www.visitaviemore.com
Food - The Dalfaber Golf and Country Club has a bar and restaurant open to the public.
Fuel Station - 1 mile south along Grampian road.

57

Aviemore to Boat of Garten

Walk Data

Orientation
Point to point

Length (one way)
6 miles (9.7kms)

Grade
● Easy

Time (one way)
2½ hours

Height Gain
Minimal

Hills & Steeps
Fairly level

Terrain
Road and tracks

Markings
► Cycle route 7

Wheelchairs
Not suitable

Access for Prams
Good all the way

Key Features

🐜 Ant Hills

🚲 Cycling Routes

⛳ Golf Course

🚂 Steam Train

Noise Indicator

🔊 Trains, golfers and some bird songs.

Walk starts from Dalfaber Country Club

This six-mile (one-way) walk between Aviemore and the Boat of Garten is a stroll along well-maintained hard tracks.

The recognised start point is at the north end of Aviemore just after the Morrison Housing estate (you can't miss Morrison's - it looks like Balamory). The track travels along a path and turns right leading to a gate. After passing through the gate, you will next go under the main line railway and over some bridges before going through a second tunnel, which is under the steam train railway line. You continue along the well-defined track that takes you through a birch wood, which runs between the first part of the Spey Valley Golf Course and the steam railway line. You follow the track through the woods until it opens out in to a moorland stretch. As the path opens up it veers away from the golf course and runs parallel with the railway line to the walk's end.

There are no big hills to tackle, with only one main incline along the golf course section. As you near Boat of Garten, you pass through a gate leading to wooded section before crossing under the rail line and on to the farm road that leads to the old station next to the Boat Hotel, where you can get refreshments.

The mid section of the walk through the birch wood is home to a very large number of rabbits, but more interestingly, if you take a close look around the base of some of the trees, you will see a number of ant colonies, which can often be two feet high - you are advised not to disturb the ants.

This is a quiet walk with only the sounds of the birds and the whistle of the steam train breaking the silence - mind you, occasionally you may hear the cries of an irate golfer as their ball lands somewhere they hadn't bargained for.

 If you walk your dog off the lead, the one main concern here is the steam railway line, which is not very well fenced off.

Location: The walks starts opposite the SNH building at the northern end of Aviemore just after the Morrison housing estate.

Extras

 Plenty of parking around Aviemore and in the Boat of Garten .

 Contact the Steam Railway to find out train services to time your walk with a train ride back to Aviemore.
www.strathspeyrailway.co.uk

 Public toilets are in the centre of Aviemore, but none along the walk.

Nearest:
Accommodation - Lots of options in Aviemore and the Boat of Garten.
visit - www.visitaviemore.com
Food - In Aviemore at the Dalfaber Country Club or in Boat of Garten at the Boat Hotel.
Fuel Station - Aviemore.

Corie Cas Lower Loop

Walk Data

Orientation
Circuit route

Length
¾ mile (1.2km)

Grade
● Easy

Time
45 minutes

Height Gain
80m (262ft)

Hills & Steeps
Steep hill

Terrain
Natural path

Markings
▶ Purple marker

Wheelchairs
No access

Access for Prams
Not suitable

Key Features

🏕 Good View points

🎿 Snowsports

🚋 Mountain Train

Noise Indicator

📢 Quiet walk unless it's windy.

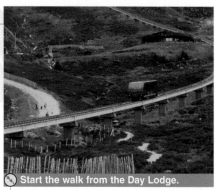
Start the walk from the Day Lodge.

The Cairngorm Mountains are located in the eastern highlands and stretch between Aviemore to the west and Braemar in the east. The area is famed for a number of reasons, such as being home to five of Scotland's highest mountains, the highest being Ben Macdhui at 4295Ft (1309m). However, there are a total of 13 mountains offering some of the most extreme hill walking in Britain and attracting experienced climbers from all over the world. Back in 1859 Queen Victoria walked up Ben Macdhui, but don't be fooled, this is a serious mountain and only expert walkers should tackle it: Queen Vis (god bless 'Er), would have had a full team of lackeys with her.

In more recent times, the Cairngorms have become famous for its snowsports during the winter months. There are a number of ski lifts and in 2001 a funicular railway was opened in order to replace the old chair lift system.

The Coire Cas Lower Loop is an easy walk that takes you up a path running close to the ski runs. You start from the marker post located at the top of the Day Lodge building. Follow the path which travels steadily up hill taking care to look out for the point where the track drops off to the left and heads under the funicular railway before joining a wide track where you can turn left down to the start, or turn right and continue up the Coire Cas Mountain Trail, which will take you to a height of 3200ft (1000m), but only do so if you are a competent hill walker equipped with correct clothing and footwear.

Ptarmigan

Despite being a very harsh mountain environment, certain species of wildlife live and breed on the high plateau, including ptarmigans, snowbuntings, and golden eagles. One of only two herds of reindeer in the UK lives up on the Cairngorms.

 Walking a dog here is possible but there is a lot going on so keep your dog under control.

Location: To reach the car park at the Day Lodge, you simply take the mountain road starting at the roundabout at the southern end of Aviemore (10 miles).

Extras

 Free parking is available at the Day Lodge car park.

 Toilets are available at various points in the Day Lodge and up at the Ptarmigan Restaurant and Visitor Centre, which you can either walk up to (long trek) or take the funicular train up.

Nearest:
Accommodation - At Glenmore, 2 miles down the mountain road. A much wider selection is available back in Aviemore 10 miles away.
visit - www.visitaviemore.com
Food - At the Day Lodge.
Fuel Station - Aviemore, 10 miles.

Coylumbridge to the Iron Bridge

Aviemore - Rothiemurchus see walk diagram on map page 46

Walk Data

Orientation
Circuit route

Length
4.5 miles (7.3 kms)

Grade
● Easy

Time
2 hours

Height Gain
60m (196ft)

Hills & Steeps
One steep part

Terrain
Hard grited road

Markings
▶ Red pointer

Wheelchairs
Not suitable

Access for Prams
Fairly good

Key Features

Thick forest & varied wildlife

Good View points

River Beanaidh

Noise Indicator

Water rush and lots of bird songs.

Walk starts from Rothiemurchus camp site

This is a superb family walk with some nice features, including breathtaking mountain views and wonderful woodlands.

The walk starts from a track which runs down the side of the Rothiemurchus camp site. There is a car park at the Larig Ghru cottage and from here you pass through a gate and follow the red marker post, keeping immediately to the right, before heading down the well-maintained hard-based track through the pine trees. Eventually you come to a gate as the path travels uphill: pass through the gate and after a short while the path opens out to reveal a stunning view of the Cairngorms. Continue along the level track as it begins to descend. After about half an hour, you will come to another gate that leads you back in to a forest section. Carry on down the path to another gate and on through the thick forest of pine on your left and scrub on your right.

Eventually you will come to a crossroads, where you turn left in to the woods and pass, on your right, Lochan Deo. Carry on down this path until you reach a fork with a sign pointing to Coylumbridge and opposite to the Larig Ghru. From here the Iron Bridge is only a few hundred yards ahead in the direction of Larig Ghru. At the bridge you can stop and have a picnic before heading back to the fork, taking the marked track through the trees back to the start point following the river line.

Chaffinch

Overall this walk offers a real sense of remoteness, but without the need to venture out into the wilderness. Throughout your walk you are serenaded with bird song, and if you keep your eyes peeled you just may spot a deer. The paths are mainly flat and in good weather very dry, but some parts can be muddy and uneven, making it tricky with a pram.

Extras

 Parking is available at the Larig Ghru Cottage or along the Cairngorms road, 500 meters for the start of the walk.

 Nearest toilets at the camp site, but ask permission to use.

 Nearest:
Accommodation - Lots in Aviemore. *visit* - www.visitaviemore.com
Food - Coylumbridge Hotel 2 mins.
Fuel Station - Aviemore, 2 miles.

 Keep dogs on the lead as this is an area with ground nesting birds, also beware of fast river at the Iron Bridge.

Contact for further details:
Rothiemurchus Visitor Centre
www.rothiemurchus.net
tel (01479) 812 345

Location: The Rothiemurchus campsite is on the Cairngorms road a few hundred yards past the Hilton Coylumbridge Hotel.

63

Craigellachie Nature Reserve Trails

Walk Data

Orientation
Circuit route

Length
2 miles (3.2 kms)

Grade
● Easy

Time
1 hour

Height Gain
130m (426ft)

Hills & Steeps
Steep hill

Terrain
Rough natural path

Markings
► Green arrow

Wheelchairs
No access

Access for Prams
Not suitable

Key Features

Birch & oak wood & varied wildlife

Good View points

Peregrine Falcons

Lochans

Noise Indicator

Loud road noise from the nearby A9.

Walk starts from Aviemore Centre play park

The Craigellachie Nature Reserve is located next to the busy A9 trunk road, making it one of the noisiest walks in the Cairngorms.

Two easy, marked trails snake their way through a mixture of mature birch, Scots pine, and a splattering of oak. Access to walks is a very easy, via the Aviemore centre play park. You walk under the A9 underpass and once through the tunnel you will see an information post showing the direction of the paths with all the area details.

The paths are well marked out and in a decent condition, although in places a bit rough and overgrown. The trail initially takes you past a lochan to a fork, from which you bear left and continue on the track, which gets steeper at around the half-mile point. Eventually you will reach the top of the walk, which offers great views across the Cairngorms.

As you descend, keep to the right-hand tracks at the forks towards a small lochan and walk along the water's side until you reach yet another fork. Here you can elect to go right, or head left and take the track alongside a small burn. A sort way on you'll come to a final fork and again have the choice to go left or right to reach the start point - the left trail is slightly longer but more interesting, taking you alongside the first lochan.

The rock faces of Craigellachie are favoured breeding grounds for peregrine falcons and you may well see them between April and July searching for food to take back to their nests.

The noise levels coming from the traffic on the A9 won't totally spoil the walk, and with an iPod you won't even hear it (full volume).

Peregrine Falcon

Keep dogs on the lead as the A9 is a fast and dangerous road, and it's not securely fenced off from the walk or the reserve.

Location: From the Aviemore centre, park near the children's play park and walk across the field towards the A9 and the underpass.

Extras

 Parking is available close to the reserve in the Aviemore Centre.

 The nearest public toilets are in the village centre near the Police station. However, with permission, toilets are available in various Macdonalds facilities close by.

 Nearest:
Accommodation - Lots in Aviemore.
visit - www.visitaviemore.com
Food - All around Aviemore.
Fuel Station - 1/4 mile away along Grampian road.

 Contact for further details:
SCOTTISH NATURAL HERITAGE Scottish Natural Heritage
www.snh.org.uk

Glenmore Forest Trail

Walk Data

Orientation
Circuit route

Length
3 miles (4.8 kms)

Grade
● Easy

Time
1½ hours

Height Gain
25m (82ft)

Hills & Steeps
Some hills

Terrain
Forest paths

Markings
▶ Yellow markings

Wheelchairs
Not suitable

Access for Prams
Some obstacles

Key Features

Thick forest &
varied wildlife

Good View points

Cycling Routes

Noise Indicator

Lots of bird songs
and woodland noise.

Walk starts from Alt Mor Car Park

This is one of those walks which seems to change after every turn. You walk on flats, up some hills, past animal graves over river crossings and via a shooting range: fascinating stuff, and a route the whole family can take with ease - kids will love it as there's lots to see and do. Pine martens are known to live in the woods and there are helpful marker posts giving plant information.

Start the walk from the Alt Mor Car Park near the Glenmore Visitor Centre, following the path with the yellow markings. After a short while you come to a fork - at this point take the left hand track and head up the hill through the trees towards Glenmore Lodge. At the top you will see a sign for the shooting range and opposite you will also see the small gravestones of pets from years past. Walk on round the graves, taking a sharp right with the path dipping down into the trees.

Carry on along the path until you reach a main junction where you turn right and walk along the path for 500 metres to another junction at which you turn left following the yellow marker posts as you go.

The path travels along a level route and eventually it opens out in to a clearing before reaching a wooden bridge, after crossing the water the yellow markings can seem a bit confusing, so the easiest thing to do is follow the left hand yellow markers as you go. A short distance on you will come to a metal bridge which eventually takes you back down into the woods and across yet another long wooden bridge. The path then runs parallel with the mountain road back down to the car park at the start.

The walk has good paths. For those pushing a pram you do have a couple of tight and bumpy spots, but nothing too daunting.

 The Forestry Commission ask you to keep dogs on the lead at all times as this is an area with ground-nesting birds.

Location: The Allt Mor Car Park is located next to the Cairngorms snow gates just past the Glenmore visitor centre.

Pine Martin

Extras

 Parking is available at the start of the walk 1/4 of a mile past the Glenmore Visitor Centre.

 Nearest toilets are Glenmore Visitor Centre 1/4 of a mile along the road.

 Nearest:
Accommodation - Camp site and Youth Hostel near the start.
visit - www.visitaviemore.com
Food - Glenmore Visitor Centre.
Fuel Station - Aviemore, 6 miles.

Contact for further details:
Glenmore Visitor Centre
www.forestry.gov.uk
tel (01479) 861 220

67

Lily Loch Walk (Lochan Mor)

Aviemore - Rothiemurchus   see walk diagram on map page 46

Walk Data

Orientation
Circuit route

Length
3 miles (4.8 kms)

Grade
● Easy

Time
1½ hours

Height Gain
Minimal

Hills & Steeps
A few easy hills

Terrain
Track and road

Markings
▶ Yellow markings

Wheelchairs
Part of the way

Access for Prams
Fairly good

Key Features

Thick forest &
varied wildlife

Lochan

Noise Indicator

Lots of bird songs
plus the odd car.

Start from Rothiemurchus Visitor Centre

The Lily Loch is one of Aviemore's hidden gems. Officially the Lochan Mor, this is a stunning and peaceful location where locals often tie the knot. Artists can often been seen at the water's side painting or sketching the wonderful scenery, which offers a mixture of pine trees, mountain views and water features.

The walk starts from a track located opposite the Rothiemurchus Visitor Centre. Behind the car park and village green, you will come to a metal gate that leads into a wood. Follow the path with its yellow markers, through the wood along a good path, but one that on a wet day could be very muddy in places. The path gradually heads up hill with a clearing to the left. Eventually the path opens out in to a clearing with great views of the Cairngorms to take in.

You follow the path back into the woods and continue until it meets a junction at which point you then turn right and travel along the track which winds through a very pleasant wooded area that is slightly hilly - but don't fret, the inclines are very gentle. Eventually you will see the Lily Loch on your left at the bottom of a small hill just over a bridge. Being such a peaceful location, the area attracts lots of birds, and as well as the sound of birdsong all around, ducks can been observed milling around on the water.

Greylag Goose

After spending some time chilling out at the waterside, you continue along the track towards Milton Cottage, at which point you turn left to the Loch an Eilein road. Continue down the tarmac road for half a mile until you reach a junction at the end of the wooded section. Here you turn left again and take the hard base road back to the start point via Black Park.

Overall this is a fairly quiet walk and one that can be done fairly easily with a child in a pram.

Keep dogs on the lead as this is an area with ground nesting birds and other wildlife.

Location: Rothiemurchus Visitor centre is a mile south of Aviemore along the Cairngorm road.

Extras

 Park at Rothiemurchus Visitor Centre or opposite next to the village green.

 Nearest toilets at the visitor centre, in the cafe/ restaurant.

 Nearest:
Accommodation - Lots in Aviemore.
visit - www.visitaviemore.com
Food - Rothiemurchus centre.
Fuel Station - Aviemore, 1 mile.

 Contact for further details:
Rothiemurchus Visitor Centre
www.rothiemurchus.net
tel (01479) 812 345

69

Loch an Eilein Circular Trail

Aviemore - Rothiemurchus   see walk diagram on map page 47

Walk Data

Orientation
Circuit route

Length
3 miles (4.8 kms)

Grade
● Easy

Time
1½ hours

Height Gain
Minimal

Hills & Steeps
Some inclines

Terrain
Natural terrain

Markings
▶ Blue markings

Wheelchairs
No access

Access for Prams
Can be bumpy

Key Features

Thick forest & varied wildlife

Cycling Routes

Castle

Loch an Eilein

Noise Indicator

Quiet walk with lots of wildlife sounds.

Walk starts from Loch an Eilein Car Park

Regarded as one of the finest family walks in the area, Loch an Eilein is a simply stunning location which has formed the backdrop for many TV programmes, thanks mostly to its mystic island's 600-year-old castle.

Located 3 miles south of Aviemore, this is a circuit walk around the loch, which can also take in the nearby Loch Gamhna. There is a well-worn path, but not always along the water's edge. It makes no real difference which way round you go, but the rule of thumb here is that as long as the loch is within easy view, you shouldn't get lost. You can either stay on the main path, with its blue marker posts or walk close to the water's edge on numerous other, smaller tracks.

Given that the terrain here is soft, on a rainy day some parts can be very muddy, and so many trees surrounding the loch there are lots of roots poking through the ground, but don't let that put you off, because this is an easy walk for all abilities and if you are pushing a pram, things are not that bad.

This is a quiet loch walk, with the only noise coming from the wind in the trees and birds singing. The legendary island of the loch's name comes with a castle which in turn comes with a hefty dose of folk lore - whatever the truth, the place makes for a great photo!

Long Tailed Tit

The loch and woods are home to lots of shy birds, mammals and fish. Ospreys are often seen flying over the water in search of supper, looking especially for pike. While it's known that Scottish crossbills, wagtails and various tits (the flying type, not politicians) hang out in the trees. Botanists are also pre-sented with lots of interesting fauna to discover, such as green shield-moss (Buxbaumia viridis).

Keep dogs on the lead as this is an area with ground nesting birds and other wildlife.

Location: from Aviemore, travel along the Cairngorm road and turn right on to the B970 for Kincraig. After a mile turn left at the loch sign and follow the road to the car park.

Extras

 Park at car park at the end of the road leading to the loch. There is a small daily fee payable on entry.

 Toilets are available at the small visitor centre close to the loch ahead of the car park.

Nearest:
Accommodation - Lots in Aviemore.
visit - www.visitaviemore.com
Food - Rothiemurchus centre.
Fuel Station - Aviemore, 3 miles.

Contact for further details:
Rothiemurchus Visitor Centre
www.rothiemurchus.net
tel (01479) 812 345

71

Loch Morlich Circular

Aviemore - Glenmore Forest   see walk diagram on map page 47

Walk Data

Orientation
Circuit route

Length
3.4 miles (5.5kms)

Grade
• Easy

Time
1½ hours

Height Gain
Minimal

Hills & Steeps
Fairly level

Terrain
Hard base

Markings
► Red markers

Wheelchairs
A short section

Access for Prams
Good all the way

Key Features

Good View points

Watersports

Cycling Routes

Loch Morlich

Noise Indicator

Forest noise coupled with people and cars.

Start from the Loch Morlich Boathouse

This is a walk which attracts walkers, cyclists, orienteers, in fact anyone who is anyone - even anoraks with £300 hi-tech walking boots (don't do it). However, it's easy to see why so many individuals are attracted to this spot, which sits at the foothills of the Cairngorms.

The well-maintained hard base path follows the loch's edge for three-quarters of the way and only veers away at a couple of sections, with the highest point along the southern stretch. However, one quarter of the walk is actually through a wood section on the opposite side of the access road and not really part of the loch at all, but is still good.

The walk can be picked up at various points, but a good start is the Boathouse where there is a car park and toilets. Initially you follow the blue, brown and white markers before picking up the red post. From the Boathouse, walk through the trees leading to a wooden bridge and after crossing, you turn right following the white posts until you come to a junction. From here turn right again and walk along the south shore following the red posts. Continue walking along the track until you reach another junction where you turn right once more in the direction of the main road. Eventually you will reach the road, which you will have to cross in order to pick up the cycle track that runs parallel with the road back to the Boathouse, which will enable you to finish the full circuit.

Mallard

Loch Morlich plays host to various watersports along the northern shores, and with a number of sandy beaches. It's a very popular family spot for picnics.

This is not a testing walk, and for families with a pram there are no worries or obstacles to climb.

The Forestry Commission ask you to keep dogs on the lead at all times as this is an area with ground-nesting birds.

Location: Loch Morlich is 6 miles east of Aviemore along the Cairngorm road.

Extras

 Parking is available costing from £1 a day. Tickets are available from the pay and display machine.

 Male and female toilets are located close to the car park, but they are not open all year round

 Nearest:
Accommodation - Camp site and Youth Hostel near the start.
visit - www.visitaviemore.com
Food - Boathouse and nearby cafe.
Fuel Station - Aviemore, 6 miles.

i Contact for further details:
Glenmore Visitor Centre
www.forestry.gov.uk
tel (01479) 861 220

Loch nan Carriagean Stone Circle

Aviemore - Rothiemurchus see walk diagram on map page 48

Walk Data

Orientation
Point to point

Length *(one way)*
2 miles (3.2 kms)

Grade
• Easy

Time *(one way)*
50 minutes

Height Gain
Minimal

Hills & Steeps
Mailnly flat

Terrain
Natural terrain

Markings
None

Wheelchairs
No access

Access for Prams
Not suitable

Key Features

Thick forest & varied wildlife

Good View points

Stone circle

Lochan

Noise Indicator

Wind rush, bird song and faint road traffic.

Walk starts from Dalfaber Country Club

This is a simple walk on the outskirts of Aviemore along good tracks to Loch nan Carriagean. At the loch- side is a stone circle feature set around a pine tree, and like all sites of this kind, it comes loaded with heaps of mumbo jumbo and folklore. Druids and other worshippers of the strange and the utterly bizarre will tell all sorts of stories explaining precisely why the stones are here. There are tales of paranoid cows on valium refusing to pass by, to witches holding medieval Ann Summers parties...

But whatever the truth, today this is simple walk that will help while away a few hours leisure time. Access the walk from the Dalfaber Golf and Country Club car park by crossing the road and taking the track through the trees next to the post-box. Follow the track past the houses and into an area of birch trees. Eventually the track reaches a gate at the golf course. Pass through it and turn left, walking around the 1st hole and 18th tee, after which you turn left and cross a bridge up to a junction, turn left and walk up the track until you come to another junction, at which point you turn right onto the Speyside Way.

Walk along the path until it the leaves the pine trees and veers away from the golf course at a route 7 sign post. On the left is an old vehicle track which takes you down to a path at the steam railway line. Turn right and continue to an old metal gate and railway crossing on your left. Cross the line turning right on to the path and walk alongside the pinewood. In front of you you'll see a fence and a gate - don't go through it, instead turn left and walk along the fence to the lochan, passing a gap on your right with a track and sign to the Boat of Garten. The site is just ahead in the heather. To return you simply retrace your steps.

 If you walk your dog off the lead, the one main concern is the steam railway line, which is not very well fenced off.

Location: Dalfaber is at the north end of Aviemore off Grampian road 500 metres over the railway line.

Black Headed Gull

Extras

Free parking is available at the Dalfaber Golf and Country Club.

The nearest toilets are in the Dalfaber Golf and Country (patrons only). Public toilets are located in the village centre.

Nearest:
Accommodation - Lots in Aviemore. visit - www.visitaviemore.com
Food - The Dalfaber Golf and Country Club has a bar and restaurant open to the public.
Fuel Station - 1 mile south along Grampian road.

Lochan nan Nathrach Trail

Aviemore - Glenmore see walk diagram on map page 48

Walk Data

Orientation
Circuit route

Length
3.4 miles (5.5 kms)

Grade
● Easy

Time
1½ hours

Height Gain
40m (131ft)

Hills & Steeps
Steep section

Terrain
Natural vehicle

Markings
No full marking

Wheelchairs
Passable

Access for Prams
Good all the way

Key Features

Thick forest & varied wildlife

Cycling Routes

Picnic Table

Lochan

Noise Indicator

Quiet walk with loud forest noise.

Walk starts from the Hayfield Car Park

This is a pleasant walk offering a sense of remoteness running along an old railway line dating back to World War One. The tracks are in excellent condition and despite the initial uphill climb the walk is very rewarding, taking you high up into the forests and then back down to the southern shores of Loch Morlich.

The best way to do this circuit walk is clockwise, to get one main hill section out of the way from the outset. Start the walk from the Hayfield Car park and access the track from the stairs which lead to a crossroad, at which point bear left and follow the red route up the hill. After a short distance the track bends to the right and crosses a concrete bridge. After the bridge is another fork with a red marker post to the right, however: at this point ignore the red marker and take the left track which shoots off up hill into the pine woods. The road continues uphill until you come to a fork with a concrete box on the left. Here take the sharp right hand track and walk back down along the road in to the woods.

Eventually you will come to Lochan nan Nathrach, which is hidden in the trees, so keep your eyes peeled, you will notice a picnic table first and the lochan after. The lochan is known locally as the Serpents' Loch due to the large number of adders that have been known to breed here in the past, but don't freak – it's not very likely you'll see one now.

Back on the track, you continue through the woods and come to a fork at the edge of Loch Morlich - here you bear right and walk back to the start point.

This is quiet walk, where deer can been seen in the trees and where a family will manage with ease, even with a pram.

 The Forestry Commission ask you to keep dogs on the lead at all times as this is an area with ground-nesting birds.

Location: The Hayfield Car Park is located next to the Cairngorm snow gates just past the Glenmore visitor centre.

Adder

Glenmore

Extras

 Parking is available at the Hayfield car park a 1/4 of a mile past the Glenmore Visitor Centre.

 Nearest toilets are Glenmore Visitor Centre 1/4 of a mile along the road.

 Nearest:
Accommodation - Camp site and Youth Hostel near the start.
visit - www.visitaviemore.com
Food - Glenmore Visitor Centre.
Fuel Station - Aviemore, 6 miles.

Contact for further details:
Glenmore Visitor Centre
www.forestry.gov.uk
tel (01479) 861 220

Loch Vaa

Walk Data

Orientation
Circuit route

Length
1.5 miles (2.4 kms)

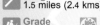
Grade
● Easy

Time
50 minutes

Height Gain
Minimal

Hills & Steeps
Small hills

Terrain
Natural earth

Markings
None

Wheelchairs
No access

Access for Prams
Not suitable

Key Features

**Thick forest &
varied wildlife**

Good View points

Lochan

Noise Indicator

Lots of loud road
traffic sounds.

Start from cemetery car park off the A95

Loch Vaa is an unassuming one, located a couple of miles north of Aviemore next to the Laggantygown Cemetery. The loch is set just off the road, but is hidden by a thick blanket of trees. You can choose to walk this circular path from either direction, it makes no difference- just remember to keep the loch close by and you won't go wrong.

There are no path signs to guide you but in most places there is a well-worn track that runs very close to the shore line. Heading round in an anti-clockwise direction, you pick up the track behind the sign at the cemetery car park where it heads up in to the trees towards the water's edge. Follow the easy path, which travels up and down small inclines and which are both narrow, and in many places, very uneven with tree roots poking through the surface and branches hanging overhead.

When there has been heavy rain the track can often be washed out: simply traverse round any water-spill and pick up the track further along.

As with other loch walks, you will often come across numerous paths near the edge, so don't worry if you stray from the original so long as you keep the loch in view, or close by. At times the track becomes overgrown with vegetation and if it's raining it can be very muddy in places.

In a couple of areas the path links up some Land Rover tracks leading to Kinveachy, and while this can form a route around the loch, it's a bit long and takes you away form the loch.

What stands out about this walk is the noise: apart for the odd bird call, at no time can you not hear the traffic on the nearby roads, which include the A9.

 Dog walkers note: you do get close to the road at the end. But otherwise no great worries.

Location: From Aviemore head north along the A95 towards Carrbridge. 2 miles out you will see the cemetery car park on the left.

Buzzard

LAGGANTYGOWN CEMETERY

Extras

 Parking is possible in the cemetery car park next to the road.

 There are no public toilets nearby. The closest being in Aviemore or in Boat of Garten 2 miles away.

Nearest:
Accommodation - Aviemore 2miles.
visit - www.visitaviemore.com
Food - Aviemore or Boat of Garten.
Fuel Station - South end of Aviemore, 3 miles from the car park at the cemetery.

Ryvoan & Green Loch Trex (Lochan Uaine)

Walk Data

Orientation
Circuit route

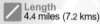
Length
4.4 miles (7.2 kms)

Grade
● Challenging

Time
2 hours

Height Gain
80m (262ft)

Hills & Steeps
Very steep

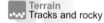
Terrain
Tracks and rocky

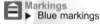
Markings
▶ Blue markings

Wheelchairs
No access

Access for Prams
Not suitable

Key Features

Thick forest & varied wildlife

Good View points

Information posts

Lochan

Noise Indicator

Lots of bird and forest sounds.

Start from behind Glenmore Visitor Centre

As a soccer fan might say, this is a walk of two halves: tough and easy, but a damn fine walk with jaw-dropping views of the Cairngorm mountains.

The first part is the tougher and not for someone on 20 cigarettes a day who suffers from vertigo! The route takes you high up and eventually leads to a rocky track which descends via a steep hill peppered with trees on a path commanding real respect. Good footwear is a must!

You start the walk from behind the Glenmore Visitor Centre and immediately head up a steep narrow hill which leads into a dark wood. At the top you turn right to the road which becomes far more manageable and dips down for a short while before heading left and going uphill again, with Scots pine lining both sides.

After a long haul up the track opens, then leaves the thick woods and mellows out, at which point your breath is taken away with the views. After a short while the road ends at a concrete box with a park bench. From here you begin the descent down a rocky path, and it's this section you'll need to take care on - test your footing, as some of the rocks can be loose.

Once you get to the bottom it's all change and the second stage of the walk, from the Green Loch, is an altogether different story. After spending some time at the Green Loch, you walk back to Glenmore along a flat and well-manicured road with information posts dotting the route back to the walk's end at the Glenmore Visitor Centre.

Although the first section of this walk is not accessible by wheelchair users or someone pushing a pram, from the Green Loch neither will have any problems at all.

 The Forestry Commission ask you to keep dogs on the lead at all times as this is an area with ground-nesting birds.

Location: The Glenmore Visitor Centre is 6 miles east of Aviemore along the Cairngorm road.

Black Grouse

Extras

 Parking is available costing from £1 a day. Tickets are available from the pay and display machine.

 Male and female toilets are located in the Glenmore Visitor centre.

 Nearest:
Accommodation - Camp site and Youth Hostel near the start.
visit - www.visitaviemore.com
Food - In the Glenmore centre or opposite in the Glenmore cafe.
Fuel Station - Aviemore, 6 miles.

Contact for further details:
Glenmore Visitor Centre
www.forestry.gov.uk
tel (01479) 861 220

The Queen's Forest Walk

Walk Data

Orientation
Circuit route

Length
4.4miles (7.2 kms)

Grade
● Easy

Time
2 hours

Height Gain
30m (98ft)

Hills & Steeps
Up hill to start

Terrain
Surfaced path

Markings
▶▶ Orange & purple

Wheelchairs
Passable

Access for Prams
Good all the way

Key Features

Thick forest &
varied wildlife

Good View points

Cycling Routes

Loch

Noise Indicator

Lots of bird songs
plus road noise.

Start from the Loch Morlich Boathouse

This is a decent family walk without any frills or trouble spots. It takes you up into the dense Queen's Forest, which forms part of the Glenmore Forest Park opposite Loch Morlich.

The route is along well-maintained paths, which mainly take you through woods with open and closed sections past the Badaguish Outdoor Centre, with the final stretch of road running alongside Loch Morlich.

The walk can be picked up at a number of points, but a good start is the Glenmore Car Park near the Boathouse. From here you cross over the road and head up the left hand track, ignoring the path signposted for walkers and cyclists. Follow the orange marker posts that take you up a long hill through an area of felled trees, which provided a clearing to give fantastic views across to the Cairngorms and down Loch Morlich.

On the first part of the walk you will encounter a fairly steep long hill, but once it flattens out there are no more major inclines to contend with and this is a walk that all ages will manage, and one that a pram can negotiate no problem.

As you pass through the woods, you will notice that in places the trees are so tightly packed that you can barely see daylight through them. They're home to all kinds of wild animals including, it's thought, even the rare and elusive wildcat, now so precious but once so common in the highlands.

Part of this walk is used for the Aviemore half marathon, so you may encounter a few athletes training for their big day (resist the urge to trip them up as they run pass...!)

Refreshments and toilets are available at the Boathouse or the nearby Glenmore Visitor Centre.

 The Forestry Commission ask you to keep dogs on the lead at all times as this is an area with ground-nesting birds.

Location: Loch Morlich is 6 miles east of Aviemore along the Cairngorm road.

Wildcat

Extras

 Parking is available costing from £1 a day. Tickets are available from the pay and display machine.

 Male and female toilets are located close to the car park, but they are not open all year round

 Nearest:
Accommodation - Camp site and Youth Hostel near the start.
visit - www.visitaviemore.com
Food - Boathouse and nearby cafe.
Fuel Station - Aviemore, 6 miles.

i **Contact for further details:**
Glenmore Visitor Centre
www.forestry.gov.uk
tel (01479) 861 220

83

The Woodland Trail

Aviemore - Glenmore Forest   see walk diagram on map page 49

Walk Data

Orientation
Circuit route

Length
1 mile (1.6 kms)

Grade
● Easy

Time
50 minutes

Height Gain
Minimal

Hills & Steeps
Falt all the way

Terrain
Surfaced path

Markings
▶ White markers

Wheelchairs
Good flat path

Access for Prams
Good all the way

Key Features

Pine trees & varied wildlife

Cycling Routes

Picnic Tables

Loch Morlich

Noise Indicator

Lots of loud bird songs.

Walk starts from the Hayfield Car Park

The Woodland Trail is set around the part of Glenmore Forest which is adjacent to Loch Morlich, at the foot of the Cairngorms, and what stands out about this very simple walk is that it's the ideal family day out, perfect for kids of all ages. There is nothing hard about the route, with only one hilly section just after the beginning, and even then it's only a gentle incline around a small wooded hill.

You start the walk from the top of the Hayfield car park, by taking a few stone steps leading you to a well- maintained path through the pine trees which line much of the way down to the loch.

A couple of minutes in, you come to a fork with a red and white marker. At this point you take the right- hand trail and walk through the trees to the next marker post, at which point you take the left-hand path following the white marker posts. After the small uphill section the path descends into an open area with stunning views of the Cairngorms to the left. As you near the loch you will see yet another white mark post, and from this point the path starts to head north for a short distance until you reach the Alt Mor waterway.

Here you can elect to finish the walk and head back to the start point following the white markers, or you can cross the waterway via the wooden bridge and turn left, following the blue markers to reach a small wooded section with picnic tables close the waters edge.

To reach the car park and finish the loop, simply walk back across the bridge and turn left following the white marker posts. Eventually you will join the first section and retrace your steps to the car park.

 The Forestry Commission ask you to keep dogs on the lead at all times as this is an area with ground nesting birds.

Location: the Hayfield car park is next to the Cairngorm snow gates just past the Glenmore visitor centre

Crested Tit

Extras

 Parking is available at the start of the walk 1/4 of a mile past the Glenmore Visitor Centre.

 Nearest toilets are Glenmore Visitor Centre 1/4 of a mile along the road.

 Nearest:
Accommodation - Camp site and Youth Hostel near the start.
visit - www.visitaviemore.com
Food - Glenmore Visitor Centre.
Fuel Station - Aviemore, 6 miles.

Contact for further details:
Glenmore Visitor Centre
www.forestry.gov.uk
tel (01479) 861 220

85

Ballater, Braemar & Dinnet

Royal Deeside is simply stunning. While so many associate this area with only the Royal Family, Balmoral Castle and Queen Victoria, there's so much more about this section of the Cairngorms National Park to savour.

Some of the longest hill walks can be found on the Grampian Mountains such as the White Mounth Munros. However, what this area is great for is its superb low-level walks spread out between Braemar, Ballater and Dinnet - where you will find the Cambus O'May Forest Trails, an excellent set of family walks with a disabled trail and a route for dogs.

The walks in and around Braemar are particularly good, and if you have the stamina then the steep hill walk up Morrone Hill will sort the boys from the men, while the Lion's Face & Cromlin walk is well worth doing.

Close to the centre of Ballater, the hill walk up Craigendarroch is a tester but well worth the effort for the views at the top. The Golf Course circular is a good family walk taking you alongside the famous River Dee.

All three areas are reached off the A93, which runs between Aberdeen and Perth, with spur roads branching off from each named village.

Ba
Br
D

Ballater Golf Course & River Dee Walk (see page 94)

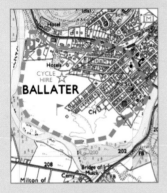

Loch Muick End View
(see page 98)

Craigendarroch Walk (see page 96)

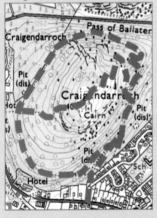

Pannanich Woods (see page 100)

Seven Bridges Walk (see page 102)

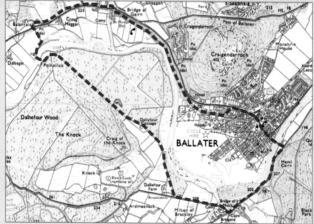

Around Craig Leek (see page 104)

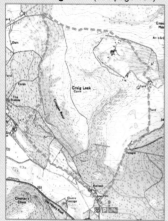

Keiloch Craig (see page 106)

Morrone Birkwood Nature Reserve (see page 108)

Morrone Hill Walk (see page 110)

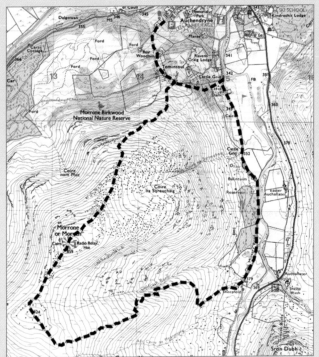

For full size maps: www.cairngormslivingwalks.com

Queen's Drive Walk (see page 112)

The Lion's Face & Cromlins Walk (see page 118)

River Dee Walk (see page 114)

Burn O'Vat Circular (see page 120)

The Creag Choinnich Walk (see page 116)

Cambus O'May Forest Trail (see page 122)

Cambus O'May Bridge & River Dee (see page 124)

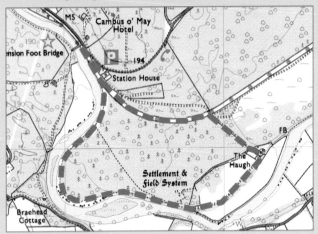

Glen Tanar Nature Reserve Walks (see page 126)

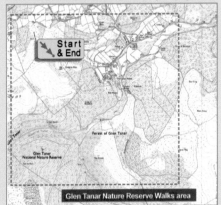

Glen Tanar Nature Reserve Walks area

For full size maps: www.cairngormslivingwalks.com

Little Ord Circular (see page 1128)

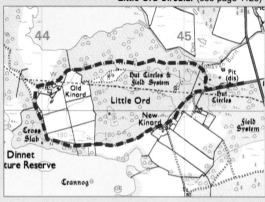

Loch Kinord Circular (see page 130)

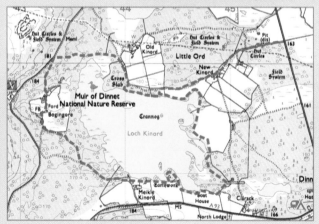

Ballater Golf Course & River Dee Walk

Walk Data

Orientation
Circuit route

Length
2 miles (3.2 km)

Grade
● Easy

Time
1 hour

Height Gain
Minimal

Hills & Steeps
Flat low level

Terrain
Surfaced & tarmac

Route Marks
► Green markers

Wheelchairs
Passable in parts

Access for Prams
Good all round

Key Features

Wood & water trail with varied wildlife

Good View points

River Dee

Noise Indicator

Golfers, water rush and road noise.

Start the walk from the village square

Around the Cairngorms National Park there are various golf course walks, and the one that follows part of Ballater's 18 hole riverside course is one of the finest. They have been playing golf here since 1892.

The walk follows an easily-navigated trail with green marker posts, and as well as running along a large part of the course, also takes you along part of the River Dee and through part of Ballater itself, forming a full circular route. If you don't want a complete circular trip, there are a series of shorter trails, which you can pick up at various points in the centre of the village or from the outskirts.

Doing the walk as a full circuit, a good start point is from the centre of Ballater at the tourist information centre. From here head down the road to the main street and cross over, turning left along the street. Passing the church on your right, you head past the shops and walk towards the river Dee and Ballater Bridge. At the bridge, bear right and walk down to the river via some steps, after which you join a path, turning right to walk through a series of gates to a caravan site. Pass through the site to the far end and look out for the marker post and track at an opening in the fence.

Hedgehog

From this point, follow the route which runs close to some of the greens before branching away and nearing the riverbank. The path is flat and well-maintained, but keep an eye out for stray golf balls heading your way, because a number of the holes neighbour the path.

Eventually you will leave the golf course and, passing a gate, you'll come to a picnic site and car park on the outskirts of Ballater. From here you simply follow the streets and roads back to the start of the walk.

Extras

 You can park at the Tourist Office or at various points around Ballater.

 There are male and female public toilets in the centre of the village.

 Since it's a golf course, and as you walk through the village along pavements, you are asked to keep dogs on a lead.

Nearest:
Accommodation - B&B's, hotels, guests houses and self catering is available all around Ballater whithin walking distance of the walk.
Food - All around Ballater
Fuel Station - There are two petrol stations in Ballater, one on the outskirts, and another along Victoria Road in the centre.

Location: The Tourist office is in the centre of Ballater.

Craigendarroch Walk

Walk Data

Orientation
Circuit route

Length
2 miles (3.2 km)

Grade
● Challenging

Time
1½ hours

Height Gain
192m (630ft)

Hills & Steeps
Steep hill

Terrain
Earth and stones

Route Marks
▶ Red markers

Wheelchairs
No access

Access for Prams
No access

Key Features

Wood & hill with varied wildlife

Good View points

Noise Indicator

Village noise coming from Ballater.

Start the walk from the village square

This is an interesting and testing hill walk rising to a summit of 402 metres - a walk with a height gain of 192 metres. It's set through an oak wood that back in the 18th Century saw its trees being chopped down to make parts for cartwheels. The oaks were grown in a process known as 'coppicing', which caused the stems to grow straight.

There are a couple of options in the way to do this walk. You can either take the less demanding circular route around the mid section of the hill, or you can turn off and do the route over the top. Either way, the walk starts out along a rough path reached off the access road, Craigendarroch Walk Road: 50 meters along on you left is a gate leading into the woods, which are quite dark in parts, and immediately the way-marked path heads up hill. Note: there is some confusion regarding the markers, because at one point you will see a wooden board telling you to follow the yellow markers for the circular route, and blue for the over the top trail, but neither seem to exist; instead there is faded red marker directing you to start off walking in a clockwise direction.

After a short while the path splits and it's here that you decide to take things easy and go around the hill, or you take the harder option and head for the summit.

The harder trail takes you up a path which eventually gets very rocky, so watch your footing, especially if the ground is damp or wet. Once you reach the top, you will find a cairn, and information board and mountain information marker. Once you have seen enough, you pick up the return path to the left of the park bench and from here you simply walk back down the path to the start point at the back of some houses.

There are no obvious worries for walking a dog off the lead once in the woods.

Location: From Station Square, walk along the A93 north passing an old church on your left. A short distance on you will come to Craigendarroch Walk Road.

Magpie

Ba

Br

D

Extras

You can park at the Tourist Office or at various points around Ballater, all very close to the start point.

There are male and female public toilets in the centre of the village.

Nearest:
Accommodation - B&B's, hotels, guests houses and self catering is available all around Ballater within walking distance of the walk.
Food - All around Ballater
Fuel Station - There are two petrol stations in Ballater, one on the outskirts and another along Victoria Road in the centre.

Lock Muick End View Circular

Ballater
see walk diagram on map page 88

Walk Data

Orientation
Circuit route

Length
2.5 miles (4.5 km)

Grade
● Easy

Time
2 hours

Height Gain
Minimal

Hills & Steeps
Flat, low level

Terrain
Hard paths

Route Marks
None

Wheelchairs
No access

Access for Prams
Passable

Key Features

Wood & water trail with varied wildlife

Good View points

Loch Muick

Noise Indicator

Very quiet & remote spot with wind noise.

Start from the Spittal of Glenmuick

Lock Muick is located in Glen Muick 7 miles south of Ballater in an area that is a nature reserve managed by the Balmoral Estate.

Around two miles long, this freshwater loch draws from Loch Allt an dubh, its waters flowing into the River Muick, which in turn joins the River Dee just outside Ballater.

Walkers have long enjoyed the glen with its long, high trails on the legendary Lochnagar and taking in Chapel Mounth en route to the Angus Glens. Queen Victoria loved it so much here that she built a small cottage called Glas-Allt Shiel, which is still in use today, at the southern end on the north side of the loch.

The walk around the north end starts from the car park and visitor centre at the Spittal of Glenmuick. From here you pass the visitor centre and buildings, going straight ahead for about half a mile until you come to a track on your right. Turn right here and go down to the loch's edge, which you stay on until you reach the boathouse and main track via a bridge. From here you turn right and walk along to a lodge at Allt-na-giubhsaich set in a small wood. Just past the building is a track on the right, which you take in order to complete the circuit at the visitor centre, where you will find information about the estate and its wildlife.

If you fancy a longer walk, there's the full circuit trail around the whole loch, which is seven and a half miles in total, taking about three and a half hours.

Red deer are common here. In summer they can be found on the higher ground, while in winter they head down to the lower areas of the glen to shelter and feed. Ring ouzels and dippers are just two of the bird species to look out for.

 Great place to walk the dog, but being a nature reserve, care and control is called for.

Location: From Ballater head south along the B976 in the direction of Glen Muick. The car is at the road end, 7 miles on.

Ring Ouzel

Ba
Br
D

Extras

 You can park a short walk from the visitors centre. There is a daily charge for cars.

 There are public toilets next to the visitor centre.

Nearest:
Accommodation - B&B's, hotels, guests houses and self catering is available in Ballater 7 miles away.
Food - In Ballater 7 miles away.
Fuel Station - There are two petrol stations in Ballater 7 miles back up the glen. One petrol ststion can be found on the outskirts of Ballater near Ballater Bridge, and another along Victoria Road.

99

Pannanich Woods

Walk Data

Orientation
Circuit route

Length
3 miles (5 km)

Grade
● Challenging

Time
1½ hours

Height Gain
197m (646)

Hills & Steeps
Long steep hill

Terrain
Natual paths

Route Marks
▶ Red arrows

Wheelchairs
No access

Access for Prams
Not suitable

Key Features

Wood & hill trail
with varied wildlife

Good View points

Noise Indicator

Forest sounds with
some vehicle noise.

Start the walk from the Ballater Bridge

Close to Ballater, overlooking the village, are the dense, hilly Pannanich Woods managed by the Forestry Commission.

Many years ago they played a vital role in helping to defeat Hitler. In 1940, as the Second World War escalated, Canadian lumberjacks from Newfoundland came to Ballater to fell trees for use in the war effort. They set up their "Glenmuick Camp" and got to work, cutting down 3000 trees a week. The camp is long gone but to find out more of the story visit www.ballaterforestry.org.uk.

This is not a mountain walk but it's still a tough hill trail, so heavy smokers forget it - and, note, good foot wear is called for, especially when it's raining.

There are two start points and two walk options: easy shortie or tough hill trek. The closest access point from Ballater is opposite Ballater Bridge, where you will find an opening with a signpost. Here simply walk up the track until you come to a wide vehicle track and a clearing. From the information board, you turn right and follow the way-markers, walking the full hill circuit in an anti-clockwise direction. The walk starts out sedate and easy, but you are soon in for a shock because once you reach the left-turn in the track, things change 100% - if you're not up to steep hill climbs, turn back now. Ahead of you it's all up and up, and you will be sweating by the time you get to the top near the radio mast. You can peel off the main track and walk up to the mast to claim your rewarding views.

Crane Fly (Daddy Longlegs)

Ba
Br
D

🐾 As in most woods, there's lots of wildlife to look out for. If you're really lucky you'll spot the increasingly rare ground-nesting capercaillie. A severely endangered species, they're most at risk between March and August, when hens will be sitting on their chicks. So be SURE to keep your dog on a lead!

Location: Start the walk a few metres opposite Ballater Bridge.

Extras

🚗 You can park around Ballater, there is also a small car park near one of the walk's start points along the South Dee Side Road one mile from Ballater.

🚻 There are male and female public toilets in the centre of the village.

📷 **Nearest:**
Accommodation - B&B's, hotels, guests houses and self catering is available all around Ballater whithin walking distabce of the walk.
Food - All around Ballater
Fuel Station - There are two petrol stations in Ballater, one on the outskirts, and another along Victoria Road in the centre.

101

Seven Bridges Walk

Ballater see walk diagram on map page 89

Walk Data

Orientation
Circuit route

Length
5 miles (8 km)

Grade
● Easy

Time
2 hours

Height Gain
Minimal

Hills & Steeps
Low level walk

Terrain
Tarmac & natural

Route Marks
▶ Blue markers

Wheelchairs
No full access

Access for Prams
Passabale in parts

Key Features

Wood & water trail
with varied wildlife

Good View points

River Dee

Noise Indicator

Noisy with lots of
cars and road noise.

Start the walk from the village square

It says Seven Bridges on the tin, and seven bridges is just what you get, but just like an over-hyped rollercoaster, don't expect the most exciting ride of your life on this walk - you'll be somewhat disappointed, to say the least, with this strange 5-mile trail which takes you north-west out of Ballater and returns from the south via the River Dee.

The main problem is having to walk along the roads in order to connect the full circuit, and apart from the straight section through Dalhefour Woods, there's no other time when you feel you're doing a quiet countryside walk, since the route is accompanied by traffic roar coming from the B972 (which you have to cross on a couple of occasions).

However, all said and done this is an easy walk and very pleasant in the main. Early on it takes you through a small oak wood and down an open pine trail, as well crossing over the River Dee twice.

Redwing

Walking anti-clockwise, start from the centre of Braemar and head up the main road, crossing an old railway bridge (1). At the converted church, turn left down Invercauld Road and pick up Dundarroch on the right, which will take you to Old Line Road, an oak wood and footbridge (2). The way-markers lead you up onto the A93 and along to a road bridge (3). Taking care to check for traffic, cross over the road and follow the markers, which soon lead you back across the road and down to a suspension bridge (4). Cross the bridge and walk through the pine woods which lead to the South Deeside Road, where you will cross over the Bridge of Muick (5) and 100 meters on you cross another small bridge (6) before reaching Ballater Bridge (7) which will take you back to the start of the walk.

Extras

You can park at the Tourist Office or at various points around Ballater.

There are male and female public toilets in the centre of the village.

Nearest:
Accommodation - B&B's, hotels, guests houses and self catering is available all around Ballater whithin walking distance of the walk.
Food - All around Ballater
Fuel Station - There are two petrol stations in Ballater, one on the outskirts, and another along Victoria Road in the centre.

Because of the roads and livestock in fields, especially near Dalhefour Woods, this not a good walk for a dog off the lead.

Location: Start from the centre of Ballater.

Around Craig Leek

Walk Data

Orientation
Circuit route

Length
5.2 miles (8.4 km)

Grade
● Moderate

Time
2½ hours

Height Gain
208m (682ft)

Hills & Steeps
Long hills

Terrain
Tarmac & natural

Route Marks
▶ Orange arrows

Wheelchairs
Tarmac section only

Access for Prams
Tarmac section only

Key Features

Forest & moorland with varied wildlife

Good View points

Abandoned Village

Noise Indicator

Wind, bird song and low flying RAF jets.

Walk starts at Invercauld Estate car park

The walk around the high and prominent hill of Craig Leek, which rises to a summit of 635m (2083ft), is very interesting for a number of reasons, but chiefly for the diversity of the terrain and landscape that you pass through, which ranges from woodlands to high open moorland.

Craig Leek lies within the Invercauld Estate just 3 miles from east of Braemar, and despite being a long walk - and one that involves a trek uphill with a height gain of over 200 metres - this is a walk that most will be able to cope with. It's not a specialist route needing fancy walking aids, overpriced gizmos or some strutting guide.

There are a number of outstanding features about this walk, none moreso than the majestic mix of trees lining the tarmac road at Invercauld House.

From the car park just off the A93, you follow the orange arrows past the estate office and head down the metalled road for about a mile, until you come to a marker post telling you to head right up into the woods. From this point the walk follows vehicle tracks for the rest of the way, all of them clearly marked.

Common Crossbill

The initial track uphill through an open forest is fairly sedate with no steep sections or obstacles to climb. After a while the path exits the woods and follows a wall into heather moorland which will take you past the remains of an old village, before taking you back through a wooded section again. The RAF practice low- level flying in the area and you may well find yourself being used as a target, so keep your head down (but don't fret - they're lousy shots).

 This is a good walk with a dog, but you are asked to keep your pooch under control at all times to protect wildlife: note that deer stalking takes place between July and February.

Location: The car park is 50m off the A93, 3 miles east of Braemar just past the old Invercauld Bridge.

Extras

 There is a car park close to the Invercauld estate office just off the A93, 200m along the road past the old Invercalud Bridge. There are daily parking charges ranging from £2.50.

 There is a single, male/female toilet at the car park.

Nearest:
Accommodation - Braemar, 3 miles away with guests houses, hotels, B&B's and self-catering homes.
Food - Braemar, 3 miles away.
Fuel Station - On the outskirts of Braemar, 3 miles from the car park at start of the walk.

Keiloch Crag

Braemar

Walk Data

 Orientation
Circuir route

 Length
3 miles (5 km)

 Grade
● Easy

 Time
1½ hours

 Height Gain
130m (427ft)

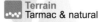 **Hills & Steeps**
Long hills

 **Terrain**
Tarmac & natural

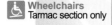 **Route Marks**
▶ Purple arrows

Wheelchairs
Tarmac section only

Access for Prams
Tarmac section only

Key Features

Forest & hill trail
with varied wildlife

Good View points

Historic Road

Noise Indicator

Bird song, low flying RAF jets and cars.

Walk starts at Invercauld Estate car park

The Keiloch Crag walk is the second of the two way-marked walks in this part of the Invervauld Estate. It's a great walk for stretching the legs and learning a bit of local history, since it includes facts about the historic road which forms part of this walk, and details on the disused limekiln set alongside the track in the woods.

To start with, the walk follows the same tarmac route as the orange trail around the Craig Leek, which initially is along a tarmac road and through some impressive tall trees. This is a family walk, but to be fair some small kids may find the high hill section a bit daunting, and indeed with a steep bank to your right as you ascend, you will need to keep children close by and the only part of this walk suitable for pushing a pram is the section running down the tarmac, which is same for wheelchair users.

106

A mile along the tarmac road from the car park, the route heads right into the woods and a few metres up you come to another marker pointing right to the pop-up information posts lining the route. From the first post the walk gradually heads uphill along a well-worn path which is wide and easy to walk on. Look out on your left for the ruin of the limekiln, which was used in the 18th century to convert limestone into fertiliser, a process known as 'slaking'. The ruin is not safe to enter.

As you walk further on, look out for the number of wind-damaged trees and the unusual shapes they have grown into, before heading on to the section of the old drove road which would have taken you to Tomintoul 300 years ago. In parts you can clearly see the early road, which once would have seen men driving their cattle to market.

 It's a good walk with a dog, but keep the beast under control in order to protect wildlife. Note that deer stalking takes place between July and February, so keep to paths.

Location: The car park is 50m off the A93, 3 miles east of Braemar just past the old Invercauld Bridge.

Kestrel

Extras

 There is a car park close to the Invercauld estate office just off the A93, 200m along the road past the old Invercalud Bridge. There are daily parking charges ranging from £2.50.

There is a single, male/female toilet at the car park.

Nearest:
Accommodation - Braemar, 3 miles away with guests houses, hotels, B&B's and self-catering homes.
Food - Braemar, 3 miles away.
Fuel Station - On the outskirts of Braemar, 3 miles from the car park at start of the walk.

Morrone Birkwood Nature Reserve

Braemar   see walk diagram on map page 90

Walk Data

 Orientation
Circuit route

 Length
3 miles (5 km)

 Grade
● Easy

 Time
1½ hours

 Height Gain
70m (230ft)

 Hills & Steeps
Level walk

 Terrain
Natural paths

 Route Marks
▶ Blue bands

Wheelchairs
No access

Access for Prams
Not suitable

Key Features

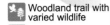 Woodland trail with
varied wildlife

Good View points

Nature Reserve

Noise Indicator

Quiet walk with only
natural sounds.

Walk starts from top of Chapel Brae road

Located within walking distance of the village centre is Morrone Birkwood Nature Reserve. It's a Special Area of Conservation as designated by the European Commission, due to its unique woodland trees and alpine plants which date back to the ice age. The birch and juniper woods are laid out on a mountain hill just above Braemar, and as well as being home to rare plants such as the globeflower (trollius) and twinflower, the reserve also sustains a herd of red deer.

The place is managed by Scottish Natural Heritage and is open all year round with no access charge, and as well as providing some excellent easy walks, it presents views which are simply stunning. The woods are said to contain our only examples of sub-alpine downy birch and juniper trees, which thrive due to the soil. The area also contains bogs, marshes and heather fields.

Access to the walks is easy, along Chapel Brae Road at the west end of the village. From the car park turn left and pass into the area following the signs. Picking up the blue marker post, you simply walk as directed, and it makes no difference if you walk clockwise or counter clockwise. The route is simple and travels along a soft path that is bumpy in places and may well be boggy in others. However, the route is not hard and you will not have to climb obstacles or wade through rivers or burns. The trail takes you through a section of trees and via heather moorland in a circular direction. There are no steep hills to conquer and located close the start of the walk is a stone mount with directions to mountains in the area, along side a park bench.

Red deer can usually be spotted around the reserve, which is surrounded by a high deer fence. There are also lots of birds chirping away, especially in the woods.

To protect wildlife, you are asked to keep dogs on a lead, or close by at all times.

Location: The car park is at the top of Chapel Brae road, which leads off from the village centre.

Red Deer

Extras

 Free parking is available at the car park at the top of the access road Chapel Brae.

 Public toilets are located in the centre of Braemar.

 Nearest:
Accommodation - Braemar, 3 miles away with guests houses, hotels, B&B's and self-catering homes.
Food - All around Braemar.
Fuel Station - 1/4 a mile from the start of the walk's car park.

109

Morrone Hill Walk

Braemar   see walk diagram on map page 90

Walk Data

Orientation
Circuit route

Length
6 miles (10 km)

Grade
● Challenging

Time
3 hours

Height Gain
490m (1,607ft)

Hills & Steeps
Very steep

Terrain
Rocks & natural

Route Marks
No way marks

Wheelchairs
No access

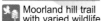
Access for Prams
Not suitable

Key Features

Moorland hill trail
with varied wildlife

Good View points

Noise Indicator

Quiet barren hill walk
with wind rush noise.

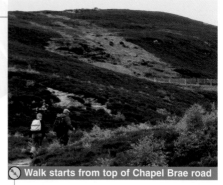
Walk starts from top of Chapel Brae road

The Morrone Hill walk is not for the fainthearted or clueless walker. For starters (well, finishers) it has a summit of 859 metres (2,818ft) - that's why the mountain rescue team used it for their telecommunications mast, and If you've never walked up a high mountain path and don't have any navigation skills, then give this one a miss, because this is the real thing.

It's within walking distance of Braemar, leading from the Morrone Birkwood Nature Reserve off Chapel Brae road or the golf course access road. Like most high regions in the Cairngorms, the weather can change very quickly, and that certainly applies to this area: should the clouds come down or the weather turn nasty you could easily find yourself disorientated, and this not a place to get lost. So you are advised to have some navigation skills and use a map for the walk, because despite having a well-defined path, the route is not way-marked.

You can do this walk as a circuit, walking up and over via the Morrone reserve, and finishing along the road that runs to the golf course, or you can simply walk up to the summit and then retrace your steps back down. However, whichever way you choose to complete the walk, a strong pair of walking boots are a must because much of the walk is along a path containing loose and embedded rocks - as you walk over them, be sure to check your footing, as many of the embedded rocks can become loose and give way.

From the start at the Morrone reserve you pass through a gate at deer fence, and immediately the walk goes uphill, but don't fret - at no time do you have to scale sheer rock faces, the path winds uphill at an even pitch, with a sharper drop down to the golf course road.

It's a good walk for a dog off the lead, with no major worries, but your dog should be healthy.

Location: The car park is at the top of Chapel Brae road, which leads off from the village centre.

Snow Bunting

Extras

Free parking is available at the car park at the top of the access road Chapel Brae.

Public toilets are located in the centre of Braemar.

Nearest:
Accommodation - Braemar, 3 miles away with guests houses, hotels, B&B's and self-catering homes.
Food - All around Braemar.
Fuel Station - 1/4 a mile from the start of the walk's car park.

Queen's Drive Walk

Braemar   see walk diagram on map page 91

Walk Data

Orientation
Circuit route

Length
3 miles (4.8 km)

Grade
● Easy

Time
1½ hours

Height Gain
50m (164ft)

Hills & Steeps
Easy hill

Terrain
Natural & tarmac

Route Marks
► Green arrow

Wheelchairs
Not suitable

Access for Prams
Passable

Key Features

Woodland trail with varied wildlife

Good View points

Noise Indicator

Woodland sounds along with car noise.

Walk starts from the centre of Braemar

The Queen's Drive Walk is a simple, low-key trail along a route said to have been popular with Queen Victoria: she would travel the path on horseback or by carriage, accompanied by her entourage.

Victoria, who was born in 1819 and reigned until 1901, fell in love with this part of Scotland and in 1852 her consort, Prince Albert, bought Balmoral Castle (6 miles from Braemar) for her. It became the royal family's summer holiday home and it still is.

Queen Victoria was married in February 1840 to her first cousin, who was born in Germany, however in 1861 Albert died of typhoid, which totally shattered her, condemning her to a mourning which resulted in her wearing black for the rest of her life. She reigned for 63 years and at her side for much of that time after Albert's death was her manservant John

Brown, who was as actually born in the small parish of Crathie, close to Balmoral Castle and 7 miles from Ballater.

The Queen's Drive Walk is a good family outing, but remember part of it is along a road. A good start point is from the centre of Braemar at the church: walk along the A93 road south out of the village in the direction of Glenshee. After half a mile you will come to a gate on your left at a marker post with a green arrow: turn left here and walk up the vehicle track which will eventually take you through a woodland and via the Corrie Feragie lochan on your left. Having walked for almost a mile you will come to the site of a derelict cottage, where in its better days Queen Victoria is said to have taken tea. There is also a sign post for Braemar, which you follow by turning left, taking the track back down to the village via a path that's a bit rough and uneven in parts.

Keep the dog on the lead along the A93 road stretch.

Location: The walk starts from the centre of Braemar next to the church of the A93 road. Look out for the sign post.

Queen Victoria

Extras

 Free parking is available at the car park opposite the Invercauld Arms Hotel 2 mins walk from the start of the walk next to the church.

 Public toilets are located in the centre of Braemar.

 Nearest:
Accommodation - Braemar has 5 hotels, 4 guests houses, 14 B&B's and some 15 self-catering homes.
Food - All around Braemar.
Fuel Station - 500 yards from the car park opposite the Invercauld Hotel on the village outskirts.

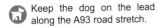

River Dee Walk

see walk diagram on map page 91

Walk Data

Orientation
Circuit route

Length
3 miles (4 km)

Grade
● Easy

Time
1½ hours

Height Gain
Minimal

Hills & Steeps
Flat walk

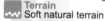
Terrain
Soft natural terrain

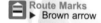
Route Marks
▶ Brown arrow

Wheelchairs
No access

Access for Prams
Not suitable

Key Features

🐾 Wood & water trail
with varied wildlife

📷 Good View points

🌊 River Dee &
Clunie Water

Noise Indicator

〰️ Water rush, birds
and the odd vehicle.

Walk starts opposite the Invercauld Hotel

The River Dee has gained its popularity thanks to the superb salmon and trout fishing that is available on one of Scotland's largest rivers, which flows from its source at the Wells of Dee high in the Cairngorm Mountains, and runs out in to the North Sea at Aberdeen passing through the Cairngorm National Park villages of Braemar, Ballater and Dinnet, a total the length of 87 miles.

The Dee is the highest sourced river in the UK, rising to almost 4000 feet (1,219m) from an area near mountain plateau of Braeriach. Every year anglers from all over the world visit the river to fish for salmon and trout in the numerous water pools and fast rapids.

The walk around the river at Braemar is very easy and will not require any great navigation skills as the walk simply follows the water's edge, firstly along the western bank of Clunie

114

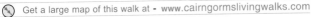

Ba

Br

D

Water and then along the southern bank of the Dee itself. The track along both rivers is a tad rough and uneven and when it's been raining the ground could be very wet and boggy in places.

Fresh Water Mussels

Start the walk from the car park opposite the Invercauld Arms Hotel. From sign post with a brown arrow cross the footbridge and turn right and walk along the narrow rough path until it meets the River Dee, at which point you turn left and walk westwards via arable land where livestock may be grazing. Eventually the river turns along a path that brings it close to the Linn of Dee road, here you can elect to walk back along the road to Braemar, or if you fancy a longer walk, continue to the Mill of Coull, before returning to the start.

Extras

The Dee and the land bordering it is home to lots of birds as well as otters, water voles and even freshwater mussels, a protected species under threat of extinction.

 Free parking is available at the car park opposite the Invercauld Arms Hotel next to the walk.

 Public toilets are located in the centre of Braemar.

 With the possibility of livestock in fields, keep your dog under control if off the lead.

Nearest:
Accommodation - Braemar has 5 hotels, 4 guests houses, 14 B&B's and some 15 self-catering homes.
Food - All around Braemar.
Fuel Station - 500 yards from the car park opposite the Invercauld Hotel on the village outskirts.

Location: The walk starts from the centre of Braemar next to the church of the A93 road.

115

The Creag Choinnich Walk

Braemar see walk diagram on map page 91

Walk Data

Orientation
Point to point

Length
2 miles (3 km)

Grade
● Challenging

Time
1½ hours

Height Gain
208m (682ft)

Hills & Steeps
Very steep hill

Start from the road behind the school

Terrain
Natural with rocks

Route Marks
▶ Red arrow

Wheelchairs
No access

Access for Prams
Not suitable

Key Features

Wood & hill trail with varied wildlife

Good View points

Noise Indicator

Woodland sounds and occasional car.

Got a couple of hours to spare and fancy a short but steep hill climb within a minute's walk for the village centre? Well look no further than this challenging hill walk to the summit of Creag Choinnich, from where you have commanding views for miles around - and a direct view down on to buildings and streets of Braemar.

Braemar is noted chiefly these days for its connection with the Royal Family, which dates back to the days of Queen Victoria when in 1852 she and her husband Prince Albert acquired Balmoral Castle, located six miles away.

The village dates back to around 1870. Before then there were two smaller villages here. The name Braemar comes from the Gaelic, Bràigh Mhàrr, meaning upland of Mar, which is the name of an area in these parts.

116

Today the village hosts one of the most popular highland games in Scotland, attended by the Queen and other members of today's Royal Family. Known as The Braemar Gathering, there has been a meet here since the time of King Malcolm Canmore some nine centuries ago.

The walk up to the hill of Creag Choinnich is a straight up and straight down again, and while it may only be a mile and quarter one way, don't be fooled. This hill will sort the men from the boys (and, of course, the women from the girls) because it's not a stroll in the park but a real hill walk. A natural soft track leads to a path with embedded and loose stones and rocks towards the summit, and for this reason a good pair of hill boots is a good idea, especially if it's been raining - the rocks can be seriously slippery. Once you have reached the summit and taken in the views, you return by retracing the climb.

 No concerns walking the dog off the lead up here.

Location: The walk starts from the centre of Braemar near the church just past the primary school.

Weasel

Ba
Br
D

Extras

 Free parking is available at the car park opposite the Invercauld Arms Hotel 2 mins walk from the start of the walk past the primary school.

 Public toilets are located in the centre of Braemar.

Nearest:
Accommodation - Braemar has 5 hotels, 4 guests houses, 14 B&B's and some 15 self-catering homes.
Food - All around Braemar.
Fuel Station - 500 yards from the car park opposite the Invercauld Hotel on the village outskirts.

117

The Lion's Face & Cromlins Walk

Braemar

see walk diagram on map page 91

Walk Data

Orientation
Circuit route

Length
2.5 miles (4 km)

Grade
● Easy

Time
1½ hours

Height Gain
100m (328ft)

Hills & Steeps
Easy hills

Terrain
Natural tracks

Route Marks
▶ Yellow band

Wheelchairs
No access

Access for Prams
Not suitable

Key Features

Wood & history trail with varied wildlife

Good View points

Historic Buildings

Noise Indicator

Woodland sounds and road noise.

Start from the road behind the school

This is a really interesting, multi-faceted walk with historic features ranging from a stately home, an ancient castle, a cottage ruin linked to Queen Victoria, a home guard world war II trench (minus Private Frazer and Captain Mainwaring) and a high rocky crag with an image of a lion said to be visible on the rock face at certain times of the year (someone's been on the wacky baccy?).

However, what makes this an interesting family walk is the diversity of its natural features. The trees are hugely fascinating, with some very intriguing shapes of all sizes, and although one part of the walk runs alongside the A93 road for a short distance, the noise of the cars doesn't detract from the enjoyment of the walk, which is lined with numerous information posts giving local history, folklore and details of plants and vegetation.

The walk starts past the primary school from the access point to the woods. Following the yellow markers, you head around the woods. After a short while you come to a junction with an information post next to the ruins of a cottage once visited by Queen Victoria. From this point you bear left along a flat part of the walk which has a fairly steep drop to your left, so keep the kids close as you pass. Ahead of you is an opening with a clear view of Invercauld House across the fields on the Invercauld Estate.

As the walk progresses, a rocky crag appears on your right. It's said that in autumn you can see the outline of a lion's head in the rock face. The path heads downhill and as you near the A93, through the trees over the road you will be able to make out Braemar Castle which dates back 1628. You also pass an old World War II trench, which was used by the Home Guard. Eventually the path heads back uphill away from the road and back into the woods to the start.

 No concerns walking a dog up here without a lead.

Location: The walk starts from the centre of Braemar near the church just past the primary school.

Brown Rat

Extras

 Free parking is available at the car park opposite the Invercauld Arms Hotel 2 mins walk from the start of the walk past the primary school.

 Public toilets are located in the centre of Braemar.

 Nearest:
Accommodation - Braemar has 5 hotels, 4 guests houses, 14 B&B's and some 15 self-catering homes.
Food - All around Braemar.
Fuel Station - 500 yards from the car park opposite the Invercauld Hotel on the village outskirts.

119

Burn O'Vat Circular

Dinnet see walk diagram on map page 91

Walk Data

Orientation
Circuit route

Length
1.3 miles (2 km)

Grade
● Easy

Time
45 minutes

Height Gain
20m (65ft)

Hills & Steeps
One small hill

Terrain
Surfaced path

Route Marks
▶ Purple arrows

Wheelchairs
No access

Access for Prams
Not suitable

Key Features

Wood & water trail with varied wildlife

Good View points

Burn O'Vat

Noise Indicator

Waterfall noise, birds and the odd car.

Start from the Muir of Dinnet Car Park

Cosily between Ballater and the hamlet of Dinnet is the Cambus O'May Forest, comprising a wide variety of trees, a loch, small lochans and ancient natural rock formations such as the Burn O'Vat.

Part of the Dinnet National Nature Reserve, the Burn O'Vat - a small cave cutting through rock with water cascading down via the Vat Burn - is well worth the slight detour on your stroll.

The hidden Vat was shaped during the Ice Age and legend has it that the cave was used to hide the 18th Century outlaw, Gilderoy Macgregor.

Getting to it is very simple, but you could get wet if the water levels are high, as you may need to scramble over some water paths to get into the vat itself.

Ba
Br
D

The walk starts from the Muir of Dinnet Car Park, which can be found of the B9119 a few miles north of Dinnet. Next to the car park is a visitor centre and from here you will see a sign for The Vat and a purple way marker. Follow the route markers down past the toilets and follow the route along a well-maintained flat path which passes through trees growing on hilly banks either side.

Brown Long-eared Bat

The walk to the Vat only takes about 10 minutes: branch off the main track and squeeze through a small opening to a point where you can view the waterfall.

THE VAT ↑

To complete the circuit, you leave the Vat and turn left over a bridge and walk uphill. The hill is steep but not long and eventually the path snakes around to a point with views across Loch Kinord and the Dinnet Nature Reserve. After taking in the scenery, you follow the path back down to the car park.

Extras

 Free parking is available next to the Visitor Centre.

 There are public toilets with baby changing facilities next to the Visitor Centre.

Walking the dog off the lead is fine as there are no farm animals to worry about.

Nearest:
Accommodation - There is a hotel at Dinnet 2¼ miles away. Ballater with a lot more options is 6 miles west of the walk and the car park
Food - Dinnet ¼ miles away.
Fuel Station - The nearest petrol station is in Ballater 6 miles away.

Location: From Dinnet take the A93 for 2 miles and turn right on to the B9119 for Strathdon. The car park is a mile ahead on the left.

121

Cambus O'May Forest Trails

Dinnet / Ballater

see walk diagram on map page 91

Walk Data

Orientation
Circuit routes

Length
Longest, 3 miles

Grade
● Easy

Time
Various

Height Gain
Minimal

Hills & Steeps
Easy long hill

Terrain
Surfaced path

Route Marks
▶▶▶▶ Various

Wheelchairs
Accessible

Access for Prams
Excellent

Key Features

Wood & water trail with varied wildlife

Good View points

Lochans

Noise Indicator

You can always hear some road noise.

Start all the walks from the Car Park

Cosily between Ballater and the hamlet of Dinnet is the Cambus O'May Forest, comprising a wide variety of trees, a loch, small lochans and ancient natural rock formations such as the Burn O'Vat., but there is even a separate walk for dogs and a trail for wheelchair users. The only downside to the walks is that the site is close to the busy A93, so for much of the time birdsong has the dubious backing of the traffic passing by. However, don't let that put you off - this forest is superb and as well as the walks there are numerous spots to picnic and lots to look out for, from lochans to wildlife.

There are four main way-marked tracks, ranging from a short 500m trail to the longest walk at 3 miles. To start with the walks are linked together, but they soon branch out to form their own routes. All the paths are well surfaced and there are no obstacles to climb.

▶The loch-side trail is a short, easy 500-metre walk with a steep start which soon mellows out. Follow the blue arrows.

▶The Auld Road Trail is a mile long walk via a lochan and through some trees. Follow green arrows.

▶The Lochan Trail is a mile-and-a-half long and takes in two small lochans. Follow the red arrows .

▶The Pine Trees Trail is a 3-mile walk. Follow the yellow arrows.

The woods are alive with birds and mammals such as red squirrels, but you'll have to keep your eyes open to see the rarer species such as Scottish crossbills and caper-caillie. Redstarts, which are also rare, nest here in the summer months having flown in from Africa.

Because of ground-nesting birds and young roe deer, you should keep your dog on a lead around the main walks, or at least very close to you. However, there is a designated dog walking area near the car park where you can let the beast run free.

Location: From Ballater take the A93 east and 3 miles out on the right, is the sign for the car park.

Redstart

Extras

 Free parking is available just off the A93 next to all of the walks

 The nearest public toilets with baby changing facilities are at the Muir of Dinnet Car Park 3 miles east along the B9119.

 Nearest:
Accommodation - Ballater has lots of accommodation options and is 2.7 miles west of the walk and the access car park.
Food - Ballater, 2.7 miles away.
Fuel Station - The nearest petrol station is in Ballater 2.7 miles away.

Ba
Br
D

123

Cambus O'May Bridge & River Dee

Dinnet see walk diagram on map page 92

Walk Data

Orientation
Circuit route

Length
2¼ miles (3.6km)

Grade
● Easy

Time
1½ hours

Height Gain
Minimal

Hills & Steeps
Low level & flat

Terrain
Natural path

Route Marks
None all round

Wheelchairs
No access

Access for Prams
Not suitable

Key Features

Wood & water trail with varied wildlife

Good View points

River Dee

Noise Indicator

Water rush coupled with vehicle noise

Start the walk from the Car Park

The River Dee is a world-famous river renowned for its fishing. Like any river, people need to be able to cross, and over the years many bridges have been constructed, not least the Cambus O'May Suspension Bridge, which spans the river 4 miles east of Ballater.

There are other bridges along the Dee close by, but the Cambus O'may crossing is the best known. The bridge was initially constructed in 1905. After a full upgrade 90 years later it was re-opened by the Queen Mother in 1988.

The bridge was built here in order to make a direct connection between Cambus O' May and the lands of Ballaterach on the southern bank of the Dee. Originally there was a ferry here to get people across but today only the bridge exists. It was cast in Aberdeen and carries walkers over the river at a point where the river bends.

To reach the bridge, walk down the steps and head west along the Deeside way. The walk, however, is in the opposite direction of the bridge, so after visiting it, you walk back along the Deeside way heading eastwards and after a short distance, and below the car park, you come to a cottage. Just past the building on your right you will see an opening with a track leading along the River Dee: head down the vehicle track and simply follow the route along side the river.

You will soon come to a fishing hut where you will find a park bench and an area where you can sit and chill for a while. Continuing along the track, the route starts to veer away from the riverside and heads up in a wood with a clearing. You keep going until you reach a site called 'The Haugh'. From here you follow the track as it bends to the left and walk on until you come to a junction. Here you turn left and rejoin the Deeside way, which will take you back to the start point.

Apart from the area near the road, there are no worries for dogs walked off the lead.

Location: From Ballater take the A93 east and 4 miles out, and on the right, is the sign for the bridge.

Ba
Br
D

Water Rail

Old Line

Extras

Free parking is available just off the A93 next to all of the walks

The nearest public toilets with baby changing facilities are at the Muir of Dinnet Car Park 2 miles north along the B9119.

Nearest:
Accommodation - Ballater has lots of accommodation options and is 4 miles west of the walk and the access car park.
Food - Ballater, 4 miles away.
Fuel Station - The nearest petrol station is in Ballater 4 miles away.

125

Glen Tanar Nature Reserve Walks

Dinnet

see walk diagram on map page 92

Walk Data

 Orientation
Circuit route

 Length
Longest is 5 miles

 Grade
● Easy

 Time
2½ hours

 Height Gain
40m (131ft)

 Hills & Steeps
Some easy hills

 Terrain
Natural

 Route Marks
▶▶▶▷▷ Various

 Wheelchairs
No access

 Access for Prams
In places

Key Features

 Wood & water trail
with varied wildlife

 Good View points

Water of Tanar

Noise Indicator

Quiet walks with only
natural sounds.

← Juniper Trail

🕐 **Start the walks from Braeloine Car Park**

Glen Tanar is 5 miles south of Dinnet. You'll discover a nature reserve managed by Scottish Natural Heritage which boasts a forest of native Scots pine said to be one of the largest of its kind.

The reserve is a working estate, but open to the public with way-marked trails for walking, cycling, horse riding and even cross country skiing in winter. The routes range from a short river trail to a 5-mile woodland walk. There are five relatively easy tracks, easy to reach and ranging over good paths from tarmac to natural and vehicular.

The longest walk is called Old Pines at 5 miles, which on average will take about two and a half hours to complete. The route starts from the car park, where you cross over an old bridge, and after turning right near the information centre you follow the green markers and head south down a stretch of road as directed. The route takes you along part of the Water of Tanar and as well as passing by and old mill, you also get to walk on an ancient right of way and pass an old chapel.

The shortest walk is the one closest to the car park called the Juniper Trail. It's a pleasant family trail with an information post telling you all about the plants and insects which can be found here, including the very rare Small Pearl-bordered Fritillary butterfly. This walk will take no longer than 20 minutes.

As well the livestock in the fields, various birds, such as Scottish crossbills and capercaille breed on the reserve, as do red squirrels. Plant lovers with a keen eye may well spot the rare twinflower.

 There is too much livestock to let the dog run amok, so keep it tethered or close by.

Location: From Dinnet head south along the B1958 and at the T-junction turn left and take the South Deeside road east until you come to the estate on the right. Pass through the gateway and head for the car park about a mile on.

Ba
Br
D

Grasshopper

Extras

 There is a pay and display car park a short walking distance from the Braeloine Visitor Centre.

 Toilets are provided at the visitor centre.

Nearest:
Accommodation - The nearest place to stay is at the Loch Kinord Hotel in Dinnet 5 miles north. www.lochkinord.com
Food - Victoria Tea Room in Dinnet
Fuel Station - On the outskirts of Dinnet on the A93 (Aboyne side).

127

Little Ord Circular

Dinnet see walk diagram on map page 93

Walk Data

Orientation
Circut route

Length
1.8 miles (3km)

Grade
● Easy

Time
1 hour

Height Gain
Minimal

Hills & Steeps
Small easy hill

Terrain
Natural path

Route Marks
▶ Blue arrow

Wheelchairs
No access

Access for Prams
Not great

Key Features

Wood & water trail with varied wildlife

Good View points

Loch Davan & Loch Kinord

Noise Indicator

Quiet walk with mainly bird song.

Start from the New Kinord Car Park

The Little Ord walk snakes round a wood which sits between two lochs, Kinord and Davan, in the Muir of Dinnet Nature Reserve.

The reserve is rich with wildlife and plants and comes loaded with historic interests, such as hut circles, a 1335 battlefield site and a Pictish stone cross dating back to the 9th century. The cross depicts a stained glass window taken from the Lesmo's Chapel in Glen Tanar, some 6 miles from here. In 1335 the battle of Culblean took place to the north of Loch Davan at the base of Culblean Hill. The battle, which played a part in the 2nd War of Succession and Independence, was fought between the English supported army of Early Davy and the troops of Sir Andrew.

This walk is neither hard nor complicated. Unless they're totally overweight or bed-ridden, anyone can do this friendly trail.

Although you can start the walk from The Burn O'Vat car park, the best place to begin is from New Kinord car park, which can be reached off the A97.

From the notice board you will see a sign directing you to head left. Following the blue arrows, walk along the wide track passing a farm on the left and through a gate. The path follows the line of the Loch Kinord walk, but after a while the red route peels away to the left and you continue straight ahead. A quarter of the way along you will come to the Pictish stone, which is fenced off to protect the site. Just past the stone cross the route changes direction and heads north before changing direction again and travels east past a ruined farmhouse at Old Kinord. As the path travels into woods you may just see Loch Davan through the trees on your left. Further on, you also pass the site of hut circles on the right, before the route heads back down to the car park.

Field Vole

This is a good walk with a dog, but note that many birds nest close to the ground.

Location: From the centre of Dinnet travel north up the A97 and turn left after 1 mile on.

Extras

Free parking is available at the start point at the New Kinord car park.

The nearest public toilets with baby changing facilities are located at the Burn O'Vat Visitor Centre 4 miles away by car, or via the walk route, about a mile and a half.

Nearest:
Accommodation - There is a hotel at Dinnet 1 mile away. Ballater with a lot more options is 8 miles west of the walk and the car park
Food - Dinnet 1 mile away.
Fuel Station - The nearest petrol station is in Ballater 8 miles away.

Loch Kinord Circular

Dinnet

see walk diagram on map page 93

Walk Data

 Orientation
Circuit route

 Length
5.3 miles (8.5km)

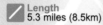 **Grade**
● Easy

 Time
2½ hours

 Height Gain
Minimal

 Hills & Steeps
Flat low lever

 Terrain
Natural paths

 Route Marks
► Red arrows

Wheelchairs
No access

Access for Prams
Not suitable

Key Features

 Wood & water trail
with varied wildlife

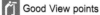 Good View points

 Loch Kinord

Noise Indicator

You can hear road
noise all the time.

Start from the Muir of Dinnet Car Park

Loch Kinord is a large loch much favoured by bird watchers and walkers alike. The loch is located in the Muir of Dinnet Nature Reserve five miles east of Ballater. There are two freshwater lochs here; Loch Davan and Loch Kinord and both support a rich array of aquatic plant life, which is one of the reasons why this area is a Designated Special Area of Conservation. The land surrounding the lochs is mainly covered in birch trees, with bogland, marshes and scrub all major features.

The walk around Loch Kinord is an easy one, even if just over 5 miles long. A good starting point is the car park at the Burn O'Vat visitor centre. Cross over the road and pick up the red marker arrows and walk as directed. At the first T-junction turn right and walk along the path through the birch wood. At this point you are a short distance away from the lochside but as you near the Parkin's Moss path and head down towards the A93 road, you will begin to near the loch along the southern shoreline.

After passing Meikle Kinord the path changes direction and as you round the loch the track veers away from it, before turning north and heading back to the shoreline again. Continue heading north following the red arrows and, ignoring the sign for New Kinord, simply bear left. Along the north section of the walk you will pass a Pictish stone dating back to the 9th century. Eventually you arrive back at the start along a route that is way-marked with various colour arrows for other walks in the area.

Geese, whooper swans, tufted ducks, golden eyes and water rails are just a few of the birds which can be seen here. Otters also live in the area and in the summer the lochs are teeming with dragonflies such as Northern Damselfly.

 This is a good walk with a dog, but remember that many birds nest close to the ground.

Location: From Dinnet take the A93 for 2 miles and turn right on to the B9119 for Strathdon. The car park is a mile ahead on the left.

Ba

Br

D

Whooper Swan

Extras

 Free parking is available next to the Visitor Centre.

 There are public toilets with baby changing facilities next to the Visitor Centre.

Nearest:
Accommodation - There is a hotel at Dinnet 2¼ miles away. Ballater with a lot more options is 6 miles west of the walk and the car park
Food - Dinnet ¼ miles away.
Fuel Station - The nearest petrol station is in Ballater 6 miles away.

Boat of Garten, Grantown-on-Spey & Nethy Bridge

The villages and towns around the northern section of the Cairngorms National Park support an array of way-marked walks, with the trails in and around Nethy Bridge some of the best looked after in the park.

There are lots of popular family walks to choose from, many following river paths such as the short river trail along the Dulnain to a bridge built by the legendary Gurkhas.

The most notable forest in the area is the Abernethy an ancient Caledonian pine treasure and now an RSPB reserve close to Loch Garten - which of course is the home to the renowned breeding pairs of osprey. The forest is also home to rare crossbill, black grouse and the almost extinct wild cat.

The Speyside Way links Boat of Garten, Nethy Bridge and Grantown-on-Spey and should you wish to walk via all three the distance is 11 miles.

For a collection of walks with a difference, then look no further than the way-marked trails on the Revack Estate. Here you will find not only good walks with lots of wildlife to look out for, but the visitor centre is first class. The family trails in the Landmark Adventure centre are also great for the younger ones.

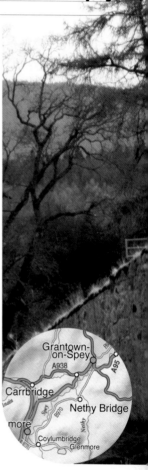

B

C

G

N

Boat of Garten to Carrbridge (see page 142)

Boat of Garten to Loch Vaa (see page 144)

For full size maps: www.cairngormslivingwalks.com

Boat of Garten Riverside Walk
(see page 146)

Boat of Garten Woodland Walks
(see page 148)

Loch Garten & Garten Woods (see page 150)

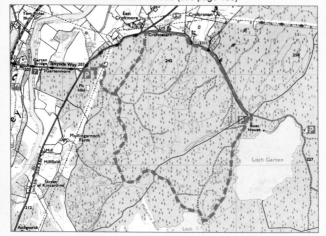

Carrbridge Circuit Trail
(see page 152)

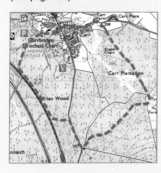

Docharn Woods Walk (see page 156)

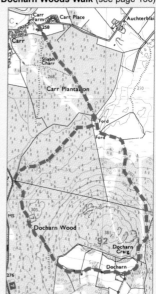

Carrbridge Woodland Trails
(see page 154)

Landmark Adventure Park
(see page158)

Sluggan Bridge Walk (see page 160)

The Gurkha Bridge Walk
(see page 162)

B

C

G

N

Anagach Woods (see page 164)

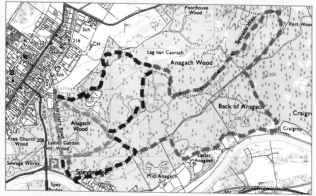

General Wade's Military Road
(see page 166)

Kylintra Meadows
(see page 170)

Grantown-on-Spey River Walk (see page 168)

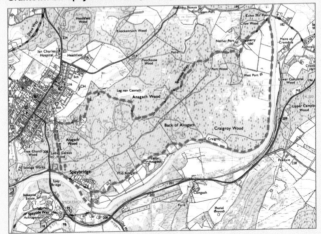

For full size maps: www.cairngormslivingwalks.com

Revack Estate Walks (see page172)

The Blue Trail, Beachen Woods
(see page 174)

Viewpoints Walk (see page 176)

Broomhill & Two Rivers Walk
(see page 180)

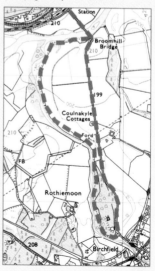

Waterfall Walk (see page 178)

B
C
G
N

Maps - by permission of Ordnance Survey
CrownCopyright Licence N0 100048399

Castle Roy Loop
(see page 182)

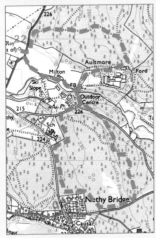

Nethy Bridge Circuit (see page 186)

Lettoch Walk (see page 184)

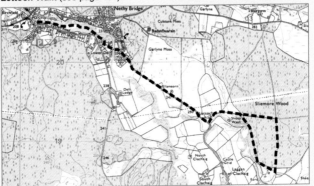

Nethy Bridge to Boat of Garten (see page 188)

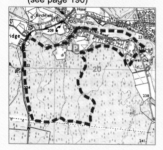

Nethy Bridge Woodland Walks
(see page 190)

B
C
G
N

Wilderness Trail
(see page 194)

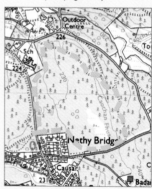

Riverside & Dell Woods
(see page 192)

Boat of Garten to Carrbridge

Boat of Garten see walk diagram on map page 134

Start walk at the end of Deshar Road

Walk Data

Orientation
Point to point

Length *(one way)*
5 miles (8kms)

Grade
● Easy

Time *(one way)*
2½ hours

Height Gain
Minimal

Hills & Steeps
Gentle inclines

Terrain
Natural paths

Markings
▶ Net work 7

Wheelchairs
No access

Access for Prams
Good all the way.

Key Features

Woodland trail with varied wildlife

Good View points

Cycling Routes

Noise Indicator

Bird songs mixed with road noise.

The walk between the Boat of Garten and Carrbridge may be 5 miles long, but you don't need to be a fitness freak to complete it, nor do you need a full outdoor gear make-over: a good pair of boots and a wetproof jacket for a rainy day will suffice.

This is a straightforward walk on hard tracks and a stretch of tarmac pavement. Start the walk from the pavement opposite the village stores along Deshar Road, which runs through the Boat of Garten. Turn right and walk down the path, which also doubles up as the Sustrans cycle route 7. Just after the primary school you come to a busy junction along the A95. Directly opposite is a farm road leading to Chapleton: taking great care, cross over the road and walk uphill, passing a number of houses and crossing a couple of cattle grids. After nearly two miles the path travels through Docharn Farm, bearing left as it goes.

Continue down the path until you reach Docharn Wood, where you go through a number of the gates (remembering to close and secure them after wards). Enter the woods and walk down the tree-lined path until you come to a junction that meets the B9153 road. At this point turn right and walk back in to the woods in the opposite direction of the main road and walk to the end of the forest.

Larry the Lamb

B

Eventually you will come to an opening in the trees and a wooden bridge. A short distance ahead is a gate that leads you back into the woods. After walking along the level track for half a mile you come to the final gate, which leads to a small car park. From here, carry on for 100 metres and then turn left on to Carr Road, which will take you down to the village centre. If you follow the Cycle route 7 markers from the off you won't go wrong.

Dogs should be kept on a lead through the farm section, as there may be lambs and other livestock around.

Location: The start of the walk is at the top end of Deshar Road near the main village shop.

Extras

Park at various points around either villages. If you are not planning to walk back, then contact one of the local taxi firms or plan your walk to time with a local bus. Daily services run between both villages.

There are no public toilets along the route, you will need to ask at hotels and other centres.

Nearest:
Accommodation - B&B's, hotels and guests houses all around Boat of Garten and Carrbridge.
visit - www.boatofgarten.com
visit - www.carrbridge.com
Food - Restaurants and a shops.
Fuel Station - In Carrbridge.

Boat of Garten to Loch Vaa

Walk Data

Orientation
Point to point

Length *(one way)*
2.5 miles (4 kms)

Grade
● Easy

Time *(one way)*
1½ hours

Height Gain
Minimal

Hills & Steeps
Small rises

Terrain
Natural paths

Markings
Sign posts

Wheelchairs
No access

Access for Prams
Okay but bump

Key Features

Wood & loch trail with varied wildlife

Good View points

Loch Vaa

Noise Indicator

Bird songs mixed with road noise.

Start walk at the end of Deshar Road

The walk between the Boat of Garten and Loch Vaa is an easy walk through a pine and birch wood along some well-defined paths lined with trees the whole way.

The initial part of the walk, which is through a local wood next to the village, can be a bit confusing due to the number of criss-crossing paths etched out over many years (possibly by loved-up locals searching for a quiet spot in the bushes), however, you shouldn't have too many problems navigating through it, and the main tracks are sign posted with place names as you go.

From the centre of the village you have a choice of starting points. You could begin by entering the woods off the Sustrans cycle track en-route to Deshar Primary School, turning left into the forest onto a track that runs west of Fairyhill.

The path leads to a junction at which point you turn right and continue along the track as it bears sharp left. After half a mile you reach a T-junction, where you turn right, following the track until it comes to a gate. Here you turn left and walk down to the loch, meeting up at a waterside hut with a fishing beat notice nailed to a tree.

The other access point in the village is from the track along Deshar Road near the station car park. This route takes you past the curling pond and in front of Fairy Hill. You follow the sign for the 'Yard', which is a mile-and-a-half ahead and takes you past a spot known as The Craigie (Creag Bheag), but a word of warning - this is a steep rock face and is not fenced off, so don't let the kids run off or throw a ball for the dog, because anyone going over the edge is not coming back. From the Yard you head right and follow the path, which takes you down to the loch as in the first route option.

 Keep the dog on a lead or close by when nearing the Craigie. The rest of the walk is fine.

Location: The start of the walk is via the woods accessed along Deshar road.

B

Sedge Warbler

Extras

 Park at the station car park or at various points around the village all within walking distance of the access woods..

 There are no public toilets, but facilities are available at the Station Hotel, ask permission.

Nearest:
Accommodation - B&B's a hotel and guests houses all around Boat of Garten, within a few minutes of the start of the trail.
visit - www.boatofgarten.com
Food - 2 restaurants and a shop.
Fuel Station - Carrbridge, 3 miles.

Boat of Garten Riverside Walk

Walk Data

 Orientation
Circuit route

 Length
2.5 miles (4kms)

 Grade
● Easy

 Time
1½ hours

 Height Gain
Minimal

 Hills & Steeps
Flat walk

 Terrain
Natural paths

 Markings
Tree sign

Wheelchairs
Not access

Access for Prams
Possible

Key Features

Wood & river trail
with varied wildlife

Good View points

River Spey

Noise Indicator

Bird songs mixed
with road noise.

Start the walks off Kinchurdy Road

It's Sunday and you spent the morning doing the normal chores: washed the car, cleaned the garage out, rearranged the potting shed, de-loused the kids, nursed a major hangover and put the bin out for the dustbin collection the following day. So come 2pm you think, what now? And having checked the TV guide only to find that there's only boring political programmes hosted by self-promoting journalists (Andrew Marr to name but one) you're left stewing...then it comes to you, what about a walk with Fido and the kids?

A riverside stroll along a short stretch of the River Spey is the perfect Sunday tonic and given that it's an easy walk with nothing to scare you and no hills to climb, even granny can come along. The walk can be picked up at any point along Kinchurdy Road, which begins opposite the Post Office in the village centre near the Boat Hotel. From there, cross the road and walk down the tarmac passing numerous houses on the left until it runs out. At this point you'll see a couple of swings, one point to the Dalvoult and another pinned to a tree pointing to Garten Bridge. From here turn left and walk down through a thin wood until you come to the steam railway crossing. Cross over and follow the track down to the river via a short field. At first the track, which can be muddy on a wet day, veers away from the riverside as it heads north passing the Boat of Garten Golf Course on the left (offer a 'fore' in a friendly greeting to the local golfers! You're sure to get a friendly wave in return!)

Eventually the path runs out and you are led up to the main road at the bridge crossing. Here turn left and walk up the road, passing the entrance to the golf club. Walk under the railway line and bear left, continuing along the pavement until you reach your start point.

 The field near the river may hold cows or other livestock, so you should keep your dog on a lead in this area.

Location: The start of the walk is opposite the Post Office along Kinchurdy road.

Pearl-Bordered Fritillary

TO GARTEN BRIDGE

B

Extras

 Park at the station car park or at various points around the village all within walking distance of the access woods.

 There are no public toilets, but facilities are available at the Station Hotel, ask permission.

Nearest:
Accommodation - B&B's a hotel and guests houses all around Boat of Garten, within a few minutes of the start of the trail.
visit - www.boatofgarten.com
Food - 2 restaurants and a shop.
Fuel Station - Carrbridge, 3 miles.

147

Boat of Garten Woodland Walks

Walk Data

Orientation
Criss crossing

Length
Up to 5 miles

Grade
● Easy

Time
Not specific

Height Gain
Minimal

Hills & Steeps
Small hills

Terrain
Surfaced paths

Markings
Sign posts

Wheelchairs
Not suitable

Access for Prams
Uneven in places

Key Features

Woodland trail with varied wildlife

Some View points

Steam Train

Rock Face

Noise Indicator

Lots of bird sounds with faint car noise.

Start the walks opposite the village shop

Close to the village centre, off Deshar Road, there's some interesting woodland comprising mature Scots pine and birch trees. While it's not dense, dark woodland there are some areas where the light strains to get through.

The woods have a number of interesting features, including a curling pond, a steep rock face and an old view-point known as Fairy Hill, not that you can see anything today - tree planting has put paid to that - but there's a sitting point at the top of what is a very small hill (not steep, easy to climb - you will not need one of those overpriced, expandable ski poles so loved by the rambler brigade).

While there are a number of main recognised paths with directions to certain place names, there are so many other short paths crisscrossing the woods that to instruct you on which to take would be pointless. The choice will be yours. But don't fret, the woods are easy to navigate and kids will love the open spaces.

There is a free local map available at the post office to will help you around the woods. The paths are natural terrain and on a wet day it will be muddy, making pram-pushing tricky. However, apart from a few spots, the paths have fairly even surfaces without too many tree roots poking through.

Various access points allow you to reach the woods and while this area is a great family spot for picnics etc, together with lots of wildlife for the kids to seek out, there is one notable feature that you should be aware of, because if you don't take care someone could get seriously hurt: the spot known as The Craigie (Creag Bheag), is a steep rock face that is not fenced off, so don't let the kids run off or throw a ball for the dog, because anyone going over the edge, is not coming back!

 Keep the dog on a lead or close by when nearing the Craigie. The rest of the walk is fine.

Location: The start of the walk is via the woods accessed along Deshar Road.

Tree Creeper

Fairy

Extras

 Park at the station car park or at various points around the village all within walking distance of the access woods.

 There are no public toilets, but facilities are available at the Station Hotel, ask permission.

Nearest:
Accommodation - B&B's a hotel and guests houses all around Boat of Garten, within a few minutes of the start of the trail.
visit - www.boatofgarten.com
Food - 2 restaurants and a shop.
Fuel Station - Carrbridge, 3 miles.

149

Loch Garten & Garten Woods

Boat of Garten

see walk diagram on map page 135

Walk Data

Orientation
Circuit route

Length
5.5miles (8.8kms)

Grade
● Easy

Time
2½ hours

Height Gain
Minimal

Hills & Steeps
Level walk

Terrain
Surfaced paths

Markings
▶ Red arrows

Wheelchairs
Good access

Access for Prams
Good all the way

Key Features

Wood & river trail with varied wildlife

Good View points

Osprey Centre

Lochs

Noise Indicator

Quiet walk with lots forest sounds.

Start the walk from Garten Woods

Loch Garten has become famous for the ospreys which have bred successfully at the RSPB reserve. Mind you, it's not just ospreys – twitchers have proliferated almost as spectacularly, binoculars glinting bright enough to rival the Hubble space probe...

There are a number of points where you can join this sedate circuit walk, winding its way around a forest of birch and Scots pine along a path which is in tip-top condition - the only time it's a bit soft is when there has been a heavy downfall.

Starting out from the Garten Woods car park near Boat of Garten, you have two initial options; with a blue route marker directing you to the Osprey Centre and the red trail taking you straight into the trees along a wide path which has a gradual incline almost from the outset.

After a short while you come to a junction, where you can elect to go left or right. Turn left and you venture towards Loch Garten. The right-hand track takes you to the much smaller Loch Mellachie. Overall this is simple family walk with no obstacles or any surprises, although some of the coloured marker posts may leave you a tad confused.

Located just north of Loch Garten is the RSPB Osprey Centre, which can be reached after a short walk down a path. The centre is open daily from 10 am to 6 pm between April and August and you can view the nest of ospreys via a combination of binoculars, telescopes and CCTV cameras. There is a small entry fee of around £3 for an adult, 50p for children.

 The forest is also home to many breeding birds such as capercaillie, crossbills, crested tits and goldeneyes, as well as the osprey, so you are asked to keep dogs on a lead during the breeding season from April to August.

Location: The Garten Woods car park is located 1/2 a mile out of Boat of Garten, directly opposite the main B970 crossroads.

Osprey

B

Extras

 Free parking is available in the Garten Woods car park. Alternatively there is free parking the the Osprey Centre.

 Public toilets with baby changing facilities and disabled toilets are available at the Osprey Centre.

 Nearest:
Accommodation - In Boat of Garten 1/4 mile from the start point.
visit - www.boatofgarten.com
Food - Boat of Garten
Fuel Station - Aviemore, 6 miles.

i **Contact for further details:**
RSPB Loch Garten
www.rspb.org.uk/reserves

151

Carrbridge Circuit Trail

Walk Data

Orientation
Circuit route

Length
3 miles (4.8kms)

Grade
● Easy

Time
1½ hours

Height Gain
Minimal

Hills & Steeps
Flat walk

Terrain
Surfaced paths

Markings
Various signs

Wheelchairs
Possible

Access for Prams
Mainly good

Key Features

Woodland trail with varied wildlife

Ant Hills

Noise Indicator

Bird songs mixed with road noise.

Start the walk along Carr Road

This is a walk which comes in two halves: it can be enjoyed as a whole walk or two separate ones. A well-defined path wraps itself around the village with the B9153 main road running through the centre and dividing the walk as it goes. Like many circuit walks, you can start it at various spots, but a good starting point is from the church.

From the church, cross over the road and walk down Carr Road, directly in front of you. Half a mile along, past the all the houses, you will come to a track off to the right alongside a field. Turn down the track and 50 meters ahead is a gate and a cycle route 7 marker post. Pass through the gate and walk into the woods along a natural path that is generally flat, mind you if there's been a downpour the path may well be muddy. The path travels into the woods in a fairly straight direction. Twenty minutes in, or a mile on, you will come to another gate, with a clearing in front of you. Pass through the gate and turn right, as directed by the path. Shortly afterwards you can cross over a small wooden bridge and immediately after that you come to a fork. At this point turn sharp right and walk back into the woods.

Another mile on the track ends at the roadside of the B9153. It's here that you can elect to shorten the walk by turning right and following the path running alongside the main road back into Carrbridge. However, if you want to complete the circuit, cross over the road and a few metres on you will see a sign directing you back in the woods. Turn left and follow the track to the railway line. The path follows the railway line and after a mile-and-a-half you will come to a junction with varying options: take the yellow marked route and walk back to the village passing along side the Landmark viewing tower.

 For dog walkers, the main concerns are the railway line, and the stretch near the road.

Location: The start of the walk is at the end of Carr Road, on the right next to the field and small un-surfaced car park.

Rabbit

C

Extras

 There is a car park in the centre of the village just up from the village Spar Shop.

 There are public toilets at the village car park close the school and playing fields.

Nearest:
Accommodation - B&B's, hotels guests houses and self-catering all around Carrbridge.
visit - www.carrbridge.com
Food - Restaurants, tea room, and a cafeteria at the Landmark Centre.
Fuel Station - In the village.

153

Carrbridge Woodland Trails

Carrbridge see walk diagram on map page 136

Walk Data

 Orientation
Criss crossing

 Length
Varying

 Grade
● Easy

 Time
Varying

 Height Gain
Minimal

 Hills & Steeps
Flat walk

 Terrain
Surfaced paths

 Markings
▶ ▶ ▶ Various

 Wheelchairs
Possible

 Access for Prams
Mainly good

Key Features

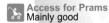 Woodland trail with varied wildlife

Ant Hills

Noise Indicator

Bird songs mixed with road noise.

Start the walks from the village hall

There are a number of things that you could say about the woodland walks area in Carrbridge, but "straightforward" isn't one of them. To call the paths and waymarkings confusing is an understatement - Professor Stephen Hawking would struggle to explain the density of these pine woods!

That said, once you have decided to go commando and take pot luck on where you might come out, the woods are actually a delight.

There are three named walks: Cairngorm View Walk, Glencharnoch Wood Walk and the Ellan Wood. All three are very similar and in certain sections at least two walks cross with each other, hence the confusion as at one point you get a post with a colour marker directing you in one direction, then up pops another pointer going the other way.

All are easily accessed from points around the village, allowing you to decided on your own start and finish point. Most of the paths are flat and even, ideal for pram-pushing, although muddy when raining, mind.

Cairngorm View Walk, waymarked in ▶red, is two miles long and will take around an hour to complete. The route takes you from the village hall to the railway line running between Perth and Inverness. The route back passes the perimeter of Landmark Adventure Park and past its wooden viewing tower.

Ellan Wood Walk, (▶ yellow marker) is, at two-and-a-half miles, the longest, taking just over an hour to finish. From the village hall, the walk snakes round towards the north of the wood via the cemetery.

The Glencharnoch (blue marker ▶) walk is the shortest (half a mile) and is circled by the Ellan walk near the cemetery.

 For dog walkers, the main concerns are the railway line, and the stretch near the road.

Location: A good start point for any of the walks is from the path near the village hall and church.

Wood Mouse

C

Extras

 There is a car park in the centre of the village just up from the village Spar Shop.

 There are public toilets at the village car park close the the school and playing fields.

Nearest:

Accommodation - B&B's, hotels guests houses and self-catering all around Carrbridge.
visit - www.carrbridge.com
Food - Restaurants, tea room, and a cafeteria at the Landmark Centre.
Fuel Station - In the village.

Docharn Woods Walk

Carrbridge

see walk diagram on map page 136

Walk Data

Orientation
Circuit route

Length
5 miles (8kms)

Grade
● Moderate

Time
2½ hours

Height Gain
40m (131ft)

Hills & Steeps
Easy hill sections

Terrain
Natural paths

Markings
▶ Cycle route 7

Wheelchairs
No access

Access for Prams
Not suitable

Key Features

Woodland trail with varied wildlife

Good View points

Ant Hills

Cycling Routes

Noise Indicator

Quiet walk with bird and wood sounds.

Start the walk from end of Carr Road

This is a good walk with a couple sections where you need to pay particular attention if you're not going to get lost. However, you are not required to wear his and hers anoraks, so don't be fooled by the overdressed rambler groups marching along two by two with their team leaders calling them to heel. You can do this walk with the minimum of fuss, but like any long walk, good footwear is required.

Start the walk form the small car park at the end of Carr road. At the gate, walk into the woods (cycle route 7) and after 20 minutes you will come to another gate. Pass through and follow the path to the right and over a bridge, which immediately leads to a fork. Here you turn right, and walk down to the B9153 road. At the junction you turn sharp left and walk up the track, which eventually comes to a clearing. Here you pass through some gates and then walk on to Docharn Farm.

Walk through the centre of the farm to the point where the track turns right at the farmhouse. Here you turn left off the main path and pick up the vehicle track running alongside a stone wall. At the top, climb over the fence and walk down into a clearing, passing under the telephone cables. You follow the path downhill as it runs parallel with the phone lines until you come to another gate, which you climb over and walk back under the phone lines walking through the birch trees and then a section of pines.

At the end of the woods the path enters a clearing with a fence in front of you. Head for the fence, but don't cross it, simply turn left and walk around until you come to a point where the fence does a sharp right. At this point walk straight on, aiming for a gate and crossing a small wooden bridge to reach it. Pass through the gate onto your outward-bound track and simply trace your steps back to the start point.

 Dogs should be kept on a lead through the farm areas, because of livestock.

Location: The start of the walk is at the end of Carr road, on the right next to the field and small car park.

Gertrude

Extras

 There is a car park in the centre of the village just up from the village Spar Shop.

 There are public toilets at the village car park close the the school and playing fields.

Nearest:
Accommodation - B&B's, hotels guests houses and self-catering all around Carrbridge.
visit - www.carrbridge.com
Food - Restaurants, tea room, and a cafeteria at the Landmark Centre.
Fuel Station - In the village.

Landmark Adventure Park Trails

Walk Data

 Orientation
Not specific

 Length
Not specific

 Grade
● Easy

 Time
Not specific

 Height Gain
Minimal

 Hills & Steeps
Simple rise

 Terrain
Surfaced paths

 Markings
Various signs

 Wheelchairs
Excellent

 Access for Prams
Excellent

Key Features

 Woodland trail with varied wildlife

 Good View points

 Ant Hills

 Adventure Rides

Noise Indicator

 Bird songs and people noise.

Start the walk from the park entrance

The Landmark Adventure Park is a very popular attraction and it's easy to see why: it's not just adventure rides and climbing walls that make this a great family place to spend the day, the centre also has a number of fun nature trails the kids love. Located in the Ancient Forest is the Red Squirrel Trail, which begins from the main entrance by following the path and bearing right where prompted. It winds its way around an area of pines and half-way round you come to the wildlife feeding area where, hopefully, you can watch the cuddly wee rodents munching away on pine seeds and other forest foods, accompanied by various birds.

The trail is a low-level walk and can be done by all ages, with good access for both wheelchair users and those with prams. It takes around 20 minutes, depending on how long you spend at the feeding area.

The Tree Top trail is an unusual walk along a wooden structure that starts at ground level but, almost imperceptibly, takes you high off the ground to give you a tree-top view of the forest at a height normally reserved for birds and squirrels. The walk splits off from the Squirrel Trail and takes around 15 minutes to complete. At the end there's a tree which was once hit by lightning and you can clearly see the scars.

Robin

The Timber Trail gives an insight into the history of logging in the highlands, with exhibitions and demonstrations. You also get to meet Lex the giant Clydesdale horse. Half-way round you come to the Fire Tower - the tallest wooden structure in Britain - and after climbing its 105 steps you have a panoramic view stretching for many miles (there's also a telescope!)

Please note, for all the trails there is an entrance fee on entering the Landmark Adventure Park.

 You are allowed to take your dogs in, but they must be kept on a lead.

Location: The centre's at the southern end of Carrbridge.

Extras

 There is a free car park next to the centre, which is set just of the main street running through Carrbridge.

 Toilets are available in the centre with baby changing facilities.

Nearest:
Accommodation - B&B's, hotels guests houses and self-catering all around Carrbridge.
visit - www.carrbridge.com
Food - There is a restaurant with a kids play area and a snack bar
Fuel Station - In the village

 Contact for further details:
www.landmark-centre.co.uk
tel: 0800731 3446

159

Sluggan Bridge Walk

Carrbridge see walk diagram on map page 137

Walk Data

Orientation
Point to Point

Length *(one way)*
2 miles (3.2kms)

Grade
● Easy

Time *(one way)*
1 hour

Height Gain
30m (98ft)

Hills & Steeps
Simple incline

Terrain
Natural & tarmac

Markings
▶ Cycle route 7

Wheelchairs
Possible

Access for Prams
Good all the way

Key Features

Wood & river trail
with varied wildlife

Good View points

Cycling Routes

Historic Bridge

Noise Indicator

Quiet with some bird
and water noise.

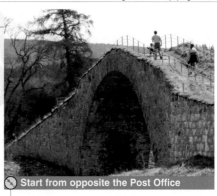

Start from opposite the Post Office

The walk to Sluggan Bridge from the centre of Carrbridge is a simple, no-nonsense one with no surprises and nothing to concern you, on tarmac first and then off-road down a natural path.

The walk is part of the national cycle route 7, and you can opt to do the trek in a number of ways. One option is the four-miles, there and back, from the centre of Carrbridge. The other is a much shorter mile-and-a-halfer from the gated path leading off the access road, which you drive to. Leave the car in a small lay-by.

Walking from Carrbridge, you begin at the Spar shop and head up Station Road, passing the historic Bridge of Carr, and walking under the railway and the busy A9 road. You continue for two miles along the tarmac road until you come to a small lay-by on the left with a gate and a cycle route 7 post. Pass through the gate and follow the well-worn track down hill through a sparse section of birch trees with a splattering of heather.

The path eventually opens out into a clearing with a house on your left and Sluggan Bridge just ahead of you spanning the River Dulnain.

Green Tiger Beatle

c

If you are really feeling energetic you can walk even further, and continue to Slochd Summit by crossing over the bridge and taking General Wade's military road for a further 3 miles, making it a 10-mile round trip from Carrbridge.

Sluggan Bridge was built back in 1729 as part of Wade's road, and today the structure is category A listed monument. In 2001 the bridge underwent major repairs by Sustrans, the transport charity, as part of the National Cycle Network.

 There are no major concerns as far as walking the dog, but it would be a good idea to keep Fido on the lead along the tarmac section, as cars do pass by.

Location: The walk starts opposite the Spar shop at the north end of the village.

Extras

 There is a car park in the centre of the village just up from the Spar Shop.

There are public toilets at the village car park close the the school and playing fields.

Nearest:

Accommodation - B&B's, hotels guests houses and self-catering all around Carrbridge.
visit - www.carrbridge.com
Food - Restaurants, tea room, and a cafeteria at the Landmark Centre.
Fuel Station - In the village.

161

The Gurkha Bridge Walk

Carrbridge see walk diagram on map page 137

Walk Data

 Orientation
Circuit route

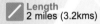 **Length**
2 miles (3.2kms)

 Grade
● Easy

 Time
40 minutes

 Height Gain
Not noticeable

 Hills & Steeps
Flat walk

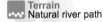 **Terrain**
Natural river path

 Markings
River sign

 Wheelchairs
No access

Access for Prams
Not suitable

Key Features

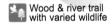 Wood & river trail
with varied wildlife

Picnic Table

Historic Bridge

Dulnain River

Noise Indicator

Road noise coming
from the A9.

Start the walk next to the petrol station

There comes a time when a long hard walk into the back of beyond is not on the menu, so an alternative simple short walk is called for, and they don't come more simple than the riverside walk which takes in the historic old packhorse bridge known as 'The Bridge of Carr'. It dates back to 1717 and is said to be the oldest stone bridge in Scotland and ends at the rather newer Gurkha Bridge built in 1992 by H Troop of the Gurkhas' 69 Squadron.

You begin the walk at the signpost next to the new road bridge and close to the garage and petrol station, which is located at the northern end of the village opposite the Carrbridge Hotel. The track drops down the riverside and you walk along the northern shore along a well-worn rough path where tree roots stick through, battling for space with stones and other natural debris.

162

The track is rather narrow in places, as well as overgrown with branches hanging low that require you to duck down to get through. A short way along, while still in the dense part of the trail, there is a field on the left where you may get to feed a carrot to the donkey and his mate.

As you progress along the trail, the path begins to open up and gets easier, not that things were especially hard to start with. Keep on the path and after 20 minutes you will come to the Gurkha bridge, which is a metal suspension with wooden floorboards. You can sit and chill at the picnic table before crossing the bridge. On the other side, you follow the path to the right and walk up to Station Road, which will take you back down to the start past a number of houses along a tarmac road.

 For dog walkers, there are no great concerns other than the river, especially if it's flowing fast after a heavy downpoor.

Location: The start of the walk is opposite the Carrbridge Hotel at the north end of the village.

E-or

Extras

 There is a car park in the centre of the village just up from the Spar Shop.

 There are public toilets at the village car park close the the school and playing fields.

Nearest:
Accommodation - B&B's, hotels guests houses and self-catering all around Carrbridge.
visit - www.carrbridge.com
Food - Restaurants, tea room, and a cafeteria at the Landmark Centre.
Fuel Station - In the village.

163

Anagach Woods

Walk Data

Orientation
Circuit route

Length
5 miles (8kms)

Grade
● Easy

Time
Various

Height Gain
Minimal

Hills & Steeps
Flat walks

Terrain
Surfaced paths

Markings
▶▶ Various

Wheelchairs
Good access

Access for Prams
Good access

Key Features

Woodland trail with varied wildlife

Cycling Routes

Golf Course

River Spey

Noise Indicator

Bird songs mixed with road noise.

Start the walk from end of Forest Road

Next to the golf course is Anagach Woods, which is said to date back to 1766 when the town was established. The woods were originally planted by the town's founder James Grant and 1000 acres of Scots pine trees adorn the area which rolls down to the Spey.

The woods are looked after by the community and managed by the Anagach Woods Trust, who maintain a network of way-marked walks which attract lots of walkers and cyclists, even dog-belt walkers leading pooches with no hands (why do they think this looks cool? Hallo...? It looks naff!). Anyway, what is not in question is the woods' appeal, where you will find three colour-coded easy walks along flat paths which you can split up and take individually, or lump together and complete as a full 5-mile outer ring circuit including a stretch of the Speyside Way.

The recognised start point for all the walks is from the entrance along Forest Road. Here you will find a notice board with details relating to all the walks and a map. The shortest walk is the green trail at 1-1/2 miles long with a walk time of 50 minutes, the blue trail, is 2 miles long taking an hour to finish, and the red walk is 5.5 miles with a time of 2-3/4 hours.

As well as the history surrounding the origins of the woods, the main path running from the car park to the river, is along the route of one of General Wade's military roads dating back to the mid 1700's.

This is a peaceful wood with several natural features shaped by the Ice Age and accordingly the flora here differs around the area. The woods are home to lots of wildlife, including chaffinches, buzzards, roe deer and even pine martens.

Should your hound have a tendency to chase little white balls, then be aware that parts of the walk are near the golf course.

Location: Access the start of the walk along Forest Road which runs past the fire station and to the south of the golf course.

Black Cap

Woodland Walks
All Routes

G

Extras

Parking is possible at the woods entrance and around the town.

Public toilets are located 5 minutes away near the museum.

Nearest:
Accommodation - A few hundred metres away around the town.
visit - www.grantownonspey.com
Food - A few hundred metres away around the town.
Fuel Station - In the town.

Contact for further details:
Anagach Woods Trust
tel: (01479) 872 273
www.anagachwoods.org.uk

General Wade's Military Road

Walk Data

Orientation
Circuit route

Length
2.5 miles (4kms)

Grade
● Easy

Time
1½ hours

Height Gain
Minimal

Hills & Steeps
Flat walk

Terrain
Natural & tarmac

Markings
Not specific

Wheelchairs
Part access

Access for Prams
Not along the river

Key Features

Wood & water trail
with varied wildlife

Good View points

Cycling Routes

River Spey

Noise Indicator

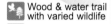
Water rush mixed
with road noise.

Start the walk from end of Forest Road

The walk along part of General Wade's military road to the old Spey Bridge is a simple one the whole family can enjoy.

The road and bridge were constructed as part of a campaign against the Highlanders. Following the Jacobite Risings in 1689 and 1715, King George decided that he had to quell any further uprisings and keep the rebellious Scots at bay, concerned that at any moment they would take up arms again. So, to establish the true nature of any further threats, in July 1724 the king despatched General George Wade to Scotland to evaluate the situation and to disarm any potential militias.

Wade, who was an Irishman born in Kilavally, reported back to the king that there was indeed a lot of unease and that Highlanders were more than capable of bearing arms and attacking the crown again. He recommended the building of garrisons, roads and bridges so that the king's troops could be moved around Scotland quickly.

In 1725 Wade began the construction of more than 250 miles of roads, with 40 bridges - and one of those roads, with its sturdy bridge, still exists at Grantown.

General Wade

The walk starts from the car park at the end of Forest Road and travels down to the River Spey along a good hard path. It's an easy walk and at the end of the woods you simply turn left and head along the river track to the old bridge, which no longer carries road traffic. However, you can walk over the bridge before returning to complete the walk back to the start, which you can select to do either by walking back along the road which leads to the bridge before turning right back in to woods, or simply by retracing your outward journey along the river track.

 For dog walkers, there are no great worries, but if Rover's not a good swimmer, note that the river is fast and deep in places.

Location: Access the start of the walk along Forest Road which runs past the fire station.

G

Extras

 Parking is possible at the woods entrance and around the town.

Public toilets are located 5 minutes away near the museum.

 Nearest:
Accommodation - A few hundred metres away around the town.
visit - www.grantownonspey.com
Food - A few hundred metres away around the town.
Fuel Station - In the town.

i Contact for further details:
Anagach Woods Trust
tel: (01479) 872 273
www.anagachwoods.org.uk

167

Grantown-on-Spey River Walk

Grantown-on-Spey see walk diagram on map page 138

Walk Data

Orientation
Circuit route

Length
7 miles (11kms)

Grade
● Easy

Time
2½ hours

Height Gain
Minimal

Hills & Steeps
Flat walk

Terrain
Natural paths

Markings
▶ Red & Speyside

Wheelchairs
Part access

Access for Prams
Not along the river

Key Features

Wood & water trail with varied wildlife

Good View points

River Spey

Noise Indicator

Water rush mixed with road noise.

Start from the Grantown Spey bridge

With a stretch of river running along the south side of Grantown, a river walk is inevitable, and this one is as good as any other along this legendary trout and salmon river: it's long been said the pools along this part of the Spey offer some of the best fishing in Scotland.

You could do the walk as a long circuit, or as a shortie around the Old Spey Bridge.

Doing the full walk, start from the small car park near the river and just off the roundabout on the approach road in to the town. From the car park walk down the path and after a short distance you will come to a junction marked with a large sign announcing the entrance to Anagach Wood. Turn left and walk into the woods along the old military road till you reach the top end near the golf course. From here follow the red marker post which runs in conjunction with the Speyside Way.

You continue along the top stretch of the walk to Mains of Cromdale, passing a small clearing, old glacial lakes and a curling rink that is used in winter.

At a point called Nether Port you continue along the Speyside Way, passing an old quarry and on until the path nears a track that would take you to a road bridge crossing the Spey. Don't walk up to the bridge, instead bear right and join the river track and, heading south, simply walk along the path which runs close to the river bank with a number clearings, but mostly trees, on your outer side. The river section is almost three miles long and on the way you pass under the old Spey bridge built by General Wade in 1754.

You are spoilt for choice when it comes to the wildlife, and often you'll spot anglers waist-deep in wait for the big one...

 For dog walkers there are no great worries, but look out for livestock around the river section.

Location: Access the start of the woods reached off the round about near the current Spey Bridge..

Smooth Newt

Extras

 Parking is possible at the woods entrance and around the town.

 Public toilets are located 5 minutes away near the museum.

Nearest:
Accommodation - A few hundred metres away around the town.
visit - www.grantownonspey.com
Food - A few hundred metres away around the town.
Fuel Station - In the town.

 Contact for further details:
Anagach Woods Trust
tel: (01479) 872 273
www.anagachwoods.org.uk

169

Kylintra Meadows

Walk Data

Orientation
Circuit route

Length
Not specific

Grade
● Easy

Time
Not specific

Height Gain
Minimal

Hills & Steeps
Flat paths

Terrain
Surfaced paths

Markings
Information boards

Wheelchairs
Good access

Access for Prams
Easy everywhere

Key Features

Wood & lochan trail
with varied wildlife

Good View points

Interesting plants

Lochan

Noise Indicator

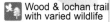
Bird song mixed
with road noise.

Enter the park off the high street

At the southern end of the Grantown, within a few minutes' walk of the town centre, has to be one of the finest centre-pieces of any of the towns or villages in the Cairngorms National Park.

Kylintra Meadows are a joy and, apart from being a place to mull away a few hours of an afternoon, the meadows are rich with plant life, not to mention birds - many of which can be seen swimming around the small lochan in the centre of the park.

While it would be perfectly okay to visit the meadows for a half-mile circuit walk - which would only take around 20 minutes - this place is an area to visit in its own right. You can stroll around all the sections in no set pattern, and on a good day with lots of sunshine this place will make the perfect setting for a picnic with the family.

Access to the meadows is possible from a number of areas within the village and at each there is a map and well-informed board giving precise details on all the features. There are also information plaques around the paths.

You are provided with details on what plants and trees to look out for and where you might find them, including common and grey alder trees, rowan (or mountain ash as it's also known), birch trees, Scots pines, hawthorn bushes, hazel, willows and gean (wild cherry) with its white blooms in summertime.

Running down the centre of the meadows is a well-tended path, running alongside a small lochan that during a cold winter and having frozen over, is used as a curling and skating rink. Lots of ducks can be seen swimming on the water with, plenty more popping in now and again for a drink and a bath.

 Highland Regional Council manages the meadows, and there are notices advising that dogs are not allowed.

Location: The meadows are opposite the Craiglynne Hotel.

Coot

Extras

 Parking is possible at the woods entrance and around the town.

 Public toilets are located 5 minutes away near the museum.

 Nearest:
Accommodation - A few hundred metres away around the town.
visit - www.grantownonspey.com
Food - A few hundred metres away around the town.
Fuel Station - In the town.

 Contact for further details:
Highland Council
tel: (01540) 661 206

G

Revack Estate Walks

Walk Data

Orentation
Circuit route

Length
Longest, 5 miles

Grade
Various

Time
Various

Height Gain
90m (295ft)

Hills & Steeps
Some steeps

Terrain
Natural paths

Markings
▶▶▶▶ Various

Wheelchairs
No access

Access for Prams
Not suitable

Key Features

Woodland trail with varied wildlife

Good View points

Picnic Tables

Noise Indicator

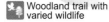
Bird song with some road noise.

All the walks start from the Visitor Centre

Few estates in the Cairngorms National Park can match this one when it comes to accessibility and facilities all under one roof, so to speak. Granted this is not the biggest highland estate in the Cairngorms National Park, but as the saying goes, it's not what you've got, it's how you use it.

Located on the estate is not only a series of waymarked trails for all abilities but also a woodland garden, a children's adventure park, a stocked lochan, a dog walking area and, to cap it all, a visitor centre which boasts a fine shop and excellent licensed restaurant.

All the walks allow you to start and finish at the car park next to the visitor centre. There are 6 named walks, which are graded - difficult, intermediate and easy - with the longest trail being around 5 miles. The red and blue trails are the easiest routes, near the visitor centre.

The blue trail is half a mile long and should take twenty minutes, while the red walk is a mile long and takes thirty minutes. The green trail, rated as intermediate, is a mile long and will take you thirty minutes do to.

Oystercatcher

The orange walk is the longest at 5 miles, but not the hardest. The trails take you around the forest above the estate and are extremely enjoyable, with tight wooded paths to open fields.

G

The yellow trail is the toughest, but probably the most enjoyable one, taking you up to the Craig Revack View point at around 1,300 feet (378m) high. The walk twists and turns all over the place, but like all the other walks, it is well marked out and easy to follow.

Around the estate you can see foxes, pheasants, red grouse, crossbills, pine martens and nesting oystercatchers.

 Dogs should be kept on a lead. There is a dog area.

Location: The Revack Estate is a mile south of Grantown, off the B970 and A95.

Extras

 Free parking at the visitor centre.

 Male and female toilets available in the visitor centre.

 Nearest:
Accommodation - A few hundred metres away around the town.
visit - www.grantownonspey.com
Food - At the visitor centre.
Fuel Station - In Grantown-on-Spey, 1 mile north.

 Contact for further details:
Revack Estate
tel: (01479) 872 234

173

The Blue Trail, Beachen Woods

Walk Data

 Orientation
Circuit route

 Length
2 miles (3kms)

 Grade
● Moderate

 Time
1½ hours

 Height Gain
80m (262ft)

 Hills & Steeps
Some steeps

 Terrain
Earth, rock, stones

 Markings
► Blue arrows

 Wheelchairs
No access

 Access for Prams
Not suitable

Key Features

 Woodland trail with varied wildlife

 Old railway line

 Old Quarry

 Railway Pond

Noise Indicator

Natural sounds of the woods.

Start walk above Grantown Caravan site

There are a number marked trails in the Beachen Woods, which vary in length but are simular in most other ways with lots of terrain variations, from soft bogs to rocky paths, pinewoods, farmland and an old railway line.

Given the nature of the terrain and the walk's location on a steep hill, good walking boots are a must up here, because one minute you are walking along a flat hard path, and the next you're knee deep in a bog. You will also be walking over some rocky outcrops, which if wet could be slippery.

The walk begins from a small car park set alongside the old railway line, which you reach by heading up left past the Grantown Caravan site and under the tunnel. The road bears left and a short way along is a side turning on the left; head down the track and this where the walk begins.

You will soon see a marker post with a series of colour arrows, green, orange and blue follow the blue arrows and when directed head up hill in to the woods along an uneven path that has roots poking through and branches hanging down. The path snakes it way up hill and keeping to the blue markings, eventually you reach a marker post in front of a stonewall where the arrows point sharp left. Follow the route down and as you descend, the track makes numerous turns along a path that can get very wet in places, at times you have to veer away form the path to avoid some bogs, you may even have to jump and few small burns.

You continue to follow the blue arrows and after walking down and around a twisting section the path enters a very dense wood before opening out on to the old railway line. At this point turn left and walk back to the start, by dropping down left on to the outward-bound track.

If you walk your dog off the lead, there are no concerns of note, but farm animals may be around.

Location: The walk starts ahead of Grantown Caravan park, 5 minutes from the town centre.

Mole

Extras

Parking is possible at the woods entrance and around the town.

Public toilets are located 5 minutes away near the town's museum.

Nearest:
Accommodation - A few hundred metres away around the town.
visit - www.grantownonspey.com
Food - A few hundred metres away around the town.
Fuel Station - In the town.

G

175

Viewpoints Walk

Walk Data

Orientation
Circuit route

Length
3 miles (5kms)

Grade
● Moderate

Time
1½ hours

Height Gain
100m (328ft)

Hills & Steeps
Steep hill

Terrain
Natural paths

Markings
▶ Yellow arrows

Wheelchairs
No access

Access for Prams
Not suitable

Key Features

Wood & water trail
with varied wildlife

Good View points

Ant Hills

Old railway line

Noise Indicator

Bird song with some
road noise at the end.

Start walk above Grantown Caravan site

The Viewpoint walk does exactly as it says on
the tin: after clambering up a long hill you're
treated to views panning out as far as the eye
can see (well, providing it's a clear day...)

The walk is well-maintained and way-marked
all the way, with posts and yellow arrows there
to point you in the right direction.

You gain access to this ramble by walking up
past the Grantown Caravan site and turning
left under the abandoned railway line. Here in
the small siding under a canopy of trees you
find some information boards with maps for the
Viewpoint and the Dava walk. Ignoring the
Dava, move through the right-hand kissing-
gate and walk up onto the old railway line. At
the top you turn left and walk along until you
come to a sign directing you to turn left.

Passing through the gate, turn right and go straight uphill crossing over a short wooden bridge and continuing up on a natural path, which is stepped with wooden runners. The walk travels through trees and along open fields and periodically there are viewing points with markers and park benches where you can catch your breath, because the uphill start is very steep and the path uneven enough to test the fittest mountain goat.

'Na' more carrots, i hate them

G

The way back is far easier, along a wide vehicle track and an old railway line. There are no obstacles to watch out for and the route is well signposted.

The walk doubles up as a bit of a nature trail, so keep your eyes peeled for buzzards soaring high above and squirrels scurrying around the forest floors. There are even signs asking you to take particular care regarding squirrels.

 There are obvious concerns for walking the dog off the lead, especially with the possibility of livestock in some of the fields.

Location: The walk starts ahead of Grantown Caravan Park, five minutes from the town centre.

Extras

 Parking is possible at the wood entrance and around the town.

 Public toilets are located 5 minutes away near the museum.

Nearest:
Accommodation - A few hundred metres away around the town.
visit - www.grantownonspey.com
Food - A few hundred metres away around the town.
Fuel Station - In the town.

177

Waterfall Walk

Grantown-on-Spey see walk diagram on map page 139

Walk Data

Orientation
Circuit route

Length
1.5 miles (2.4kms)

Grade
● Moderate

Time
1½ hour

Height Gain
110m (361ft)

Hills & Steeps
Steep hill

Terrain
Natural & tarmac

Markings
One sign

Wheelchairs
No access

Access for Prams
Not suitable

Key Features

Wood & water trail with varied wildlife

Good View points

Waterfall

Noise Indicator

Water rush mixed with natural sounds.

Start walk above Grantown Caravan site

Although not a long walk, this is a trek which will have you sweating a little by the time you make the top - and if you're stinging your lungs with 20 fags a day forget it, you're not going to manage the first hill. That said, it's a good walk, but it could be rather wet on a rainy day, so good footwear is required.

The waterfall, which is rather hidden in a crag, starts via a gate reached after a short walk up from the Grantown Caravan site. Having passed under the disused railway line, you turn right at the sign for the Viewpoint Walk. In front of you are two gates and an information board. Pass through the gate on the left and walk up the right-hand track, which begins immediately to climb uphill, with a fence running alongside on the left. As you walk you can hear the water but can't always see it, however a short way up you will come to a viewing platform which lets you get closer.

Once you've had your water rush, leave the platform and turn left continuing up the hill along the path, which is stepped out with wooden runners.

Initially the path travels through a wood, before running through a clearing with the burn still on your left as you head up. Eventually the path takes you to a farm at the top, which you will see on your right. From here you make your way round to the entrance track for the farm and follow it along for a few hundred metres until you come to a junction. Turn left and walk down the road passing another farm on your right. The steep tarmac road winds its way back to the start point, with fields either side to begin with and trees to finish. After a number of left and right-hand turns you join up with the start point just before the railway tunnel which you went under earlier.

Male Pheasant

G

Extras

Parking is possible at the wood entrance and around the town.

Public toilets are located 5 minutes away near the museum.

Nearest:
Accommodation - A few hundred metres away around the town.
visit - www.grantownonspey.com
Food - A few hundred metres away around the town.
Fuel Station - In the town.

Because the walk is around farmland, dogs should be kept on a lead or close by to protect livestock, especially during the lambing season which is usually around April each year.

Location: The walk starts ahead of Grantown Caravan Park, five minutes from the town centre.

Broomhill & Two Rivers Walk

Nethy Bridge

see walk diagram on map page 139

Walk Data

Orientation
Circuit route

Length (combined)
3 miles (4.8 kms)

Grade
● Easy

Time (combined)
1½ hours

Height Gain
Minimal

Hills & Steeps
Flat walk

Terrain
Natural & tarmac

Markings
► Red arrow

Wheelchairs
No access

Access for Prams
Not suitable

Key Features

Wood & river trail with varied wildlife

Steam Train

River Nethy

River Spey

Noise Indicator

Water rush mixed with road noise.

Start walk from opposite the Post Office

The walk along the river to Broomhill is a simple low-level one along a path that's quite often uneven, very bumpy and in some parts, completely washed out. When there has been a heavy rainfall, the path is often flooded and impassable. Signs are often posted to show if any part of the walk is closed off due to flooding and busting of the river banks.

The walk takes you along the final stretch of the River Nethy to the point where it flows in to the much larger Spey, which is famous for its salmon and trout fishing.

Heading away from the village centre towards Broomhill, you walk down the road past the butchers and old railway station on your right. A hundred metres on, you come to a left turn, which is the entrance for the water works. To the left is an opening and you will see the river on your right, the path running alongside, sticking close the shore-line. The path is rather uneven in places and, even though it is an easy family walk, you'll struggle with a pram, as there are ground roots and stiles to get over.

After walking along the river for a mile and a half, the river Nethy comes to an end and joins the Spey. At this point the path turns sharp right and heads on to the main road bridge spanning the river. From here, walk up to the bridge via a stile and cross over to reach The Broom Steam Railway Station (popular with TV audiences as Glen Bogle in The Monarch of the Glen).

This is a tranquil walk with only birdsong and the rush of water to listen to, although you will occasionally hear a car pass by on the nearby road, taking traffic between Nethy Bridge, Grantown-on-Spey and Dulnain Bridge.

 Because of the rivers and the possibility of livestock in nearby fields, dogs should be kept close or on the lead.

Location: The walks begin a few hundred meters from the village centre just past the butchers and old railway station.

Salmon

N

Extras

 There is free parking in and around Nethybridge, with parking available close to the start of the walk.

 Public toilets are located at the Abernethy Visitor Centre.

 Nearest:
Accommodation - B&B's, hotels guests houses and self-catering.
visit - www.nethybridge.com
Food - Local shop and hotels.
Fuel Station - Grantown, 9 miles.

 Contact for further details:
Explore Abernethy Visitor Centre, tel: 01479 821565.

181

Castle Roy Loop

Walk Data

Orientation
Circuit route

Length
3.5miles (5.2kms)

Grade
• Easy

Time
1 hour 45 mins

Height Gain
Minimal

Hills & Steeps
Some inclines

Terrain
Natural paths

Markings
► Pink arrow

Wheelchairs
Not suitable

Access for Prams
Not suitable

Key Features

Woodland trail with varied wildlife

Castle Roy

Allt Mor Burn

Noise Indicator

Forest noise mixed with some car noise.

Start from the car park near the castle

The Castle Roy circuit walk can be split into two small or one longer but, whichever you choose, a good starting point is from the car park next to the castle and church. Following the marker post from the car park, cross over the road and, ignoring the road to Milton, turn left onto the grass path and walk uphill for a few hundred meters, until you come to a gate at the wood's outer edge.

Pass through the gate and walk on until you come to the main track, where you turn right into the woods indicated by signposts with RSPB 'care of wildlife' notices. Walk up the woodland path, which immediately goes uphill. After a short while the path levels out before gradually going downhill. The path travels around the woods and after a short while you walk down behind some houses - including Aultmore, which is reputedly owned by Bob Dylan, the poet reputed to be a singer.

The path comes out at a burn with a bridge, and this is where you split the walk. Cross the bridge for the longer walk, or turn right for the shorter trail along the Milton road, which leads back to the castle.

The longer walk takes you around another part of the woods before looping back up to bring you past the school and the adventure centre, joining up with the small bridge again, which you cross over before turning left back to the castle car park.

Castle Roy, or Redcastle, dates back to around 1226 and is located at the north end of the village. The castle is said to be of the oldest in Scotland and today stands as a ruin, with only the walls remaining - in parts seven feet thick and 25 feet high. The castle is open to the public, but as it is unsafe you are asked to keep out.

 Because of breeding and ground nesting birds, you are also asked to keep dogs on a lead during the breeding season from April to August.

Location: The castle car park is a mile north of the village centre along the B970.

Hoverfly

N

Extras

 There is free parking in and around Nethybridge, with paring available close to the start of the walk.

 Public toilets are located at the Abernethy Visitor Centre.

 Nearest:
Accommodation - B&B's, hotels guests houses and self-catering.
visit - www.nethybridge.com
Food - Local shop and hotels.
Fuel Station - Grantown, 9 miles.

Contact for further details:
Explore Abernethy Visitor Centre, tel: 01479 821565.

Lettoch Walk

Walk Data

Orientation
Circuit route

Length
5 miles (8kms)

Grade
● Easy

Time
2½ hours

Height Gain
Minimal

Hills & Steeps
Flat walk

Terrain
Track and road

Markings
▶ Black arrows

Wheelchairs
Good access

Access for Prams
Good access

Key Features

Wood & river trail
with varied wildlife

Good View points

River Nethy

Dorback Burn

Noise Indicator

Forest noise mixed
with some car noise.

Start walk from opposite the Post Office

There are no great surprises on this walk - you won't do a sudden left turn to find yourself staring at a 20 foot wall climb with a 90 foot drop down in to a bog. No, this is your classically simple walk but note, if you smoke 60 a day and drink 15 pints of Guinness a night you'll probably be making great use of the park benches along the way. Despite being uncomplicated, this is still a five-miler...

It starts opposite the Abernethy Visitor Centre from the marker post. Following the black arrows, you walk along a very good path which will comfortably carry a wheelchair and make light work of pushing a pram. The path winds along, passing a bird feeding station before it eventually comes out at a fork at the Black Bridge, which in fact is green (someone should have gone to B&Q for a mix and match paint pot). However, following the black arrow cross-over the suspension bridge spanning the Dorback burn, walk up the short track to the road. Turn right along the road to Lettoch.

A mile and a half on, you will come to another bridge spanning the burn – this one was originally built by German prisoners of war – but don't cross it. Turn left and walk up the path into to the woods via a gate on your left. The path travels in a fairly straight line in an uphill direction through the trees. Eventually you will come to a crossroad at which you turn right and walk down and out of the woods into a field which will give you a wonderful view of the Cairngorms. Turn right onto the farm track and follow it round and over a cattle-grid to the point where you start retracing your steps back to the village.

The wood has an abundance of wildlife, including crossbills, wag-tails, robins and squirrels. Shy roe deer can also be seen in trees.

 Keep your dogs close if off the lead, and around the woods remember there may be ground-nesting birds

Location: The walks begin from the Post office, in the centre of the village next to the bridge..

Pied Wagtail

N

Extras

 There is free parking in and around Nethybridge, with parking available close to the start of the walk.

 Public toilets are located at the Abernethy Visitor Centre.

 Nearest:
Accommodation - B&B's, hotels guests houses and self-catering.
visit - www.nethybridge.com
Food - Local shop and hotels.
Fuel Station - Grantown, 9 miles.

i Contact for further details:
Explore Abernethy Visitor Centre, tel: 01479 821565.

185

Nethy Bridge Circuit

Nethy Bridge see walk diagram on map page 141

Walk Data

Orientation
Circuit route

Length
6.2 miles (10 kms)

Grade
● Moderate

Time
2½ hours

Height Gain
Minimal

Hills & Steeps
Some inclines

Terrain
Surfaced path

Markings
▶ Brown route

Wheelchairs
Not suitable

Access for Prams
Good in parts

Key Features

Wood & river trail with varied wildlife

Cycling Routes

Castle Roy

Noise Indicator

Forest noise mixed with some car noise.

Start the walk from the old station

The walk around Nethy Bridge takes you north, to a point where you could almost forget you're anywhere near the place.

In the centre of the village, start the walk from the old train station just after the information board. The first stretch of this long walk, along the Speyside Way, takes you past open farm land, a small wood and the ruins of Castle Roy on your right.

After two miles and having passed through a number of gates, you come to a bridge tunnel. Go through it and immediately turn right up the siding on to a farm track. At the top, turn left and walk down to the B970, where you turn right in the direction of Nethy Bridge along the grass path which runs parallel to the main road. After 100 metres you have to cross over the road and continue along another grass path, until you reach the number 8-marker post. A few yards ahead is a fork with a sign - follow the directions to Nethy Bridge and walk into the woods until you reach another junction. Ignoring the small right-hand track, go straight on and eventually you will come to another junction, where you turn left and join the Castle Roy and Wilderness trail.

When the track emerges from the trees and runs alongside the road, you will soon come to a small car park. From here you can choose to walk back down in to the village along the tarmac road, or stay on the path. After a short distance you come to a gate next to a road. Cross the road and walk into the Balnagowan Woods, which will lead you back to the centre of the village near the golf course and Nethy Bridge Hotel.

 The first half of the walk along the Speyside Way is fenced off, so you can let the dog run free, but working your way back through the forest you're asked to keep it on the lead, to protect breeding birds, especially between April and August

Location: The walk begins from the Post Office in the centre of the village next to the bridge.

Wood Pigeon

N

Extras

 There is free parking in and around Nethybridge, with parking available close to the start of the walk.

 Public toilets are located at the Abernethy Visitor Centre.

Nearest:
Accommodation - B&B's, hotels guests houses and self-catering.
visit - www.nethybridge.com
Food - Local shop and hotels.
Fuel Station - Grantown, 9 miles.

 Contact for further details:
Explore Abernethy Visitor Centre, tel: 01479 821565.

187

Nethy Bridge to Boat of Garten

Nethy Bridge

see walk diagram on map page 141

Walk Data

Orientation
Point to point

Length *(one way)*
5 miles (8kms)

Grade
• Moderate

Time *(one way)*
2 hours

Height Gain
Minimal

Hills & Steeps
Flat walk

Terrain
Track and tarmac

Markings
♣ White Thistle

Wheelchairs
Possible

Access for Prams
Good all the way

Key Features

Woodland trail with varied wildlife

Good View points

Ant Hills

Cycling Routes

Noise Indicator

Peaceful walk with bird song.

Start walk from opposite the Post Office

The walk between Nethy Bridge and Boat of Garten is as straightforward as it is straight, and if you get lost doing this walk then you shouldn't be allowed out on the streets.

The route follows a mainly straight section of the Speyside Way along tarmac and off-road tracks. There is nothing hard about this five-mile trek, which should take around 2 hours one way. If you're planning to walk back then you obviously need to give yourself 4 hours.

Start from the Post Office and walk along the main road in the direction of Boat of Garten. After a short while the road bends to the right and on the left is a smaller road signposted for Tulloch. Turn left down the road and past the houses is a path on the left. Walk for a few hundred metres until you see an opening across the road on the right, with a pole gate giving access to the Speyside Way.

Following the white Scottish thistle marker post, pass the notice board and walk straight ahead, passing a track on your left and a small lochan behind some trees. Follow the path through a woodland bog area until you come to a main junction - at this point turn right and walk along the track which becomes more dense with pines as you go.

Fox

After about a mile you will come to a junction. Turning left, you walk the half-mile stretch until you come to yet another junction which joins a path running alongside the tarmac road leading to Loch Garten. Turn right, and when the path stops at the road cross over and turn right to follow the route into the Boat of Garten, passing a small car park and crossing over the B970 down to the bridge that spans the River Spey. Just over the bridge is the golf club and ahead is the steam railway, walk under and turn left to reach the village centre.

 Because of breeding and ground nesting birds, you are asked to keep dogs on a lead during the breeding season from April to August.

Location: Start from the Post office in the centre of the village.

Extras

 There is free parking in and around Nethybridge, with parking available close to the start of the walk.
To get back to Nethy Bridge contact a local taxi company. There is also a local bus service runing between both villages.

Public toilets are located at the Abernethy Visitor Centre.

Nearest:
Accommodation - B&B's, hotels guests houses and self-catering.
visit - www.nethybridge.com
Food - Local shop and hotels.
Fuel Station - Grantown, 9 miles.

N

189

Nethy Bridge Woodland Walks

Nethy Bridge see walk diagram on map page 141

Walk Data

Orientation
Circuit route

Length
4 miles (6.4 kms)

Grade
• Easy

Time
1½ hours

Height Gain
Minimal

Hills & Steeps
Mostly level

Terrain
Natural paths

Markings
▶▶▶ Various

Wheelchairs
Part suitable

Access for Prams
Mostly passable

Key Features

Woodland trail with varied wildlife

Good View points

Ant Hills

River Nethy

Noise Indicator

Forest noise mixed with some car noise.

Start walk from opposite the Post Office

There are various waymarked walks in and around Nethy Bridge, including those encompassing the Kings Road Mill and Puggy Line trails located in woods behind the post office.

You could do the woodland walk as one long circuit or split it into smaller walks. As a single walk, going anti-clockwise, set off down the road next to the Abernethy Visitor Centre. Walk up the road for 100 metres and turn right for Culvardie. Keeping to the right, at the road end you join a path which leads to a road junction. Turn left here and go down Tulloch road. After some houses you leave the road, joining the path running parallel to a felled forest section. About half a mile on you'll come to a junction - turn right opposite the Speyside Way to Boat of Garten. Follow the path round and, 300 metres ahead near the burn, you come to a junction. Turn right (blue marker) and continue straight ahead until you come to another junction, at which point turn left and walk down in to the Lower Dell.

The path joins up with the river walk, which has green markers. Follow the green and blue arrows down to the river, where you turn left and walk back to the start point. The paths in the lower dell along the green trails are fine for wheel chairs and prams, but the paths in the Puggy Line Trail are not suitable, and on a wet day can be rather muddy.

The walk takes you through a section of Abernethy Forest - an important RSPB nature reserve and said to be the largest Scots pine wood in the UK. The forest is also home to a wide variety of birds and mammals, including the rare Scottish crossbills, black grouse, capercaillie and the highly elusive wild cat.

 Because of breeding and ground nesting birds, you are asked to keep dogs on a lead during the breeding season from April to August.

Location: The walk begins from the Post office, which is in the centre of the village next to the bridge.

©Capercaille

N

Extras

 There is free parking in and around Nethybridge, with parking available close to the start of the walk.

 Public toilets are located at the Abernethy Visitor Centre.

Nearest:
Accommodation - B&B's, hotels guests houses and self-catering.
visit - www.nethybridge.com
Food - Local shop and hotels.
Fuel Station - Grantown, 9 miles.

i Contact for further details:
Explore Abernethy Visitor Centre, tel: 01479 821565.

Riverside & Dell Woods Walk

Nethy Bridge see walk diagram on map page 141

Walk Data

Orientation
Circuit route

Length
2 miles (3kms)

Grade
● Easy

Time
45 minutes

Height Gain
Minimal

Hills & Steeps
Flat walk

Terrain
Natural & surfaced

Markings
▶ Green arrows

Wheelchairs
Good access

Access for Prams
Good all the way

Key Features

Wood & river trail
with varied wildlife

Ant Hills

Cycling Routes

River Nethy

Noise Indicator

Forest, water with
some car noise.

Start walk opposite the Post Office

The walk along the River Nethy and through the woods of the Lower Dell is as easy as they come, and if you can't handle this mild, basic ramble you may be in need of some medical attention. This is a fine family walk.

The River Nethy runs through the centre of the village before joining the River Spey a few miles north at Broomhill, which is on the outskirts of Nethy Bridge. While the river is not seriously deep it can flow fast.

In the centre of the village is a narrow road bridge spanning the river and from the south bank opposite the Post Office there is a small village green with a notice board and park benches. Some 20 metres along you will see a series of wooden signs with directions for individual walks. Following the green arrow: you walk along the well-maintained path close the river's edge lined with trees.

After passing a bird and squirrel-feeding table, the path heads away from the river taking you up a road. At the junction with a suspension bridge, you bear right and continue until you come to a crossroads - cross over and walk down the woodland path in to Lower Dell.

Follow the clearly-marked green arrows and eventually you'll come out onto a road. Turn right and walk to the junction, then turn left to bring you out at the Abernethy Visitor Centre.

The woods are home to plenty of wildlife: keep quiet and you just may see a deer or a crested tit, and if you're really lucky, a shy pine marten may put in an appearance. On the ground the forest floor is crawling with bug life, especially with wood ants which can be seen carrying pine needles back to their nest (which you must not disturb).

 Because of breeding and ground-nesting birds, you're asked to keep dogs on a lead during the breeding season from April to August.

Location: The walk begins from the Post office, in the centre of the village next to the bridge.

Blackbird

N

Extras

 There is free parking in and around Nethybridge, with parking available close to the start of the walk.

 Public toilets are located at the Abernethy Visitor Centre.

 Nearest:
Accommodation - B&B's, hotels guests houses and self-catering.
visit - www.nethybridge.com
Food - Local shop and hotels.
Fuel Station - Grantown, 9 miles.

i Contact for further details:
Explore Abernethy Visitor Centre, tel: 01479 821565.

Wilderness Trail

Nethy Bridge see walk diagram on map page 141

Walk Data

 Orientation
Circuit route

 Length
1½ miles (2.4kms)

 Grade
● Easy

 Time
1 hour

 Height Gain
Minimal

 Hills & Steeps
Some inclines

 Terrain
Rough earth

Markings
▶ Yellow arrows

Wheelchairs
No access

Access for Prams
Not suitable

Key Features

Wood & water trail
with varied wildlife

Ant Hills

Burns

Noise Indicator

Forest noise mixed
with some car noise.

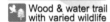 Start walk at Balnagown Wood car park

Don't let the name mislead you: this is not a far-flung wood set deep in the hills, miles from civilisation. Far from it. Much of the walk runs close to homes and their local school, whose children helped compile a highly descriptive leaflet for the wood (copies of which are available at the Abernethy Visitor Centre, near the post office).

However, what you do find here is a woodland walk that's wilder and more rugged than many of the other trails around Nethy Bridge. In parts the paths can be very uneven, with tree roots stick through. Paths swing all over the place and, as they are laid out on natural terrain and not topped with any surface material, the tracks can be very muddy and in places very boggy after the rain. And yet this all goes to make it a fun and interesting walk through tall pines, aspen, willow, juniper and silver birch.

A good start point is from the Balnagown Wood near Causer. From the car park, cross over the road and follow the yellow arrow marker posts. It makes no difference whether you go clockwise or anti clockwise, the lie of the land is the same and apart from some gentle inclines there are no worrying steeps to haul up, or any sharp turns with sudden drops. The are a number of burns to cross, some of which you need to take care with, as some of the small bridges are precisely that – indeed, one of the crossings is barely wider than a tooth pick...

The woods give shelter to a wide variety of wildlife: lurking in the trees are foxes, roe deer, squirrels, rabbits, even otters, but alas you won't see Bugs Bunny, rushing around hotly pursued by Elmer Fudd, or Daffy Duck trying to sell a raincoat to a squirrel. Still, to compensate just look up and you may be lucky and spot a crossbill.

 If you walk your dog off the lead, keep it under control and remember at times you walk near some roads.

Location: The walk begins opposite Balnagown car park, near Causer Crossroads.

Tawny Owl

N

Extras

 There's free parking in and around Nethybridge, with parking available close to the start of the walk.

 Public toilets are located at the Abernethy Visitor Centre.

 Nearest:
Accommodation - B&B's, hotels guests houses and self-catering. visit - www.nethybridge.com
Food - Local shop and hotels.
Fuel Station - Grantown, 9 miles.

Contact for further details:
Explore Abernethy Visitor Centre, tel: 01479 821565.

195

Glenlivet / Tomintoul, Strathdon

In the north of the Cairngorms National Park is the Crown Estate of Glenlivet and the small village of Tomintoul, the highest village in the Scottish Highlands.

A Crown Estate is land is owned by the sovereign, who until the reign of George III received all its rent and profits. Nowadays any profit the estate makes goes to the government.

Glenlivet is located in the shadow of the hills of Cromdale in the west and the Ladder hills in the east, and you will find some truly wonderful walks here, from high hill trails to short woodland strolls. The area is simply stunning and it offers a mixture of well-maintained farmland, major forest plantations and mountain moors -what stands out is just how well the estate maintains its way-marked walks. There are lots of well-placed sign posts, notice boards with maps and - unique for this area - a large number of conveniently named car parks at the start of most of the numbered walks.

One note of caution: most of the walks are on arable farmland, so letting your dog off the lead is not a good idea, unless you have full control of it.

G
S

Braes Heritage Trail
(see page 202)

Clash Wood (see page 206)

Bochel Circuit
(see page 204)

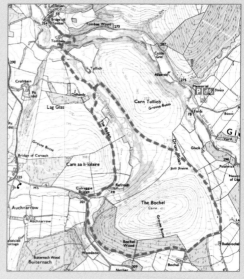

Drumin Circular & Castle Walk (see page 208)

Glen Brown - Kylnadrochit (see page 210)

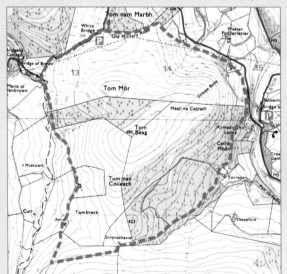

G

Glenconglass to Carn Daimh (see page 212)

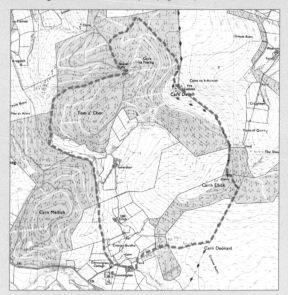

Glenmulliach Forest Nature Trail
(see page 214)

Knock Earth House -
West Avonside (see page 216)

For full size maps: www.cairngormslivingwalks.com

Tom Dubh Wood Walk
(see page 218)

Ben Newe Forest Walks
(see page 222)

Tomnavoulin - Carn Daimh Circuit (see page 220)

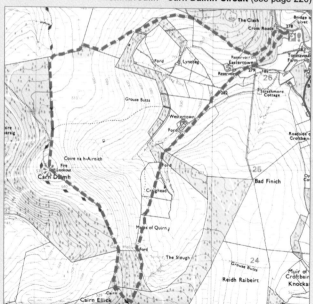

G

Braes Heritage Trail

Glenlivet / Tomintoul see walk diagram on map page 198

see walk diagram on map page 198

Walk Data

Orientation
Circuit route

Length
4 miles (6.4 km)

Grade
● Moderate

Time
1½ hours

Height Gain
230m (755ft)

Hills & Steeps
Long steep hill

Terrain
Natural paths

Markings
Walk number 2

Wheelchairs
No access

Access for Prams
No access

Key Features

Open moorland with varied wildlife

Good View points

Historic Site

Whisky Distillery

Noise Indicator

Lots of bird sounds and wind rush.

Start the walk from Eskemulloch Car Park

In an area of hilly farmland behind the Braeval Whisky Distillery, this open moorland walk known as The Braes Heritage Trail takes in Scalan, an ancient catholic site, and a trip to the view point on the top of the hill known as Tom Trumper at 582m (1909ft), from which there are stunning long off views across the Ladder Hills, to Slochdburn, the Cairngorms and the Braes of Glenlivet. You can also look down on the Braeval Distillery.

The Scalan is a building which was used as a seminary, or college, in order for worshipers of the catholic faith to carry on their trade, so to speak. The site dates back to 1717, and remained intact until around 1746, when it was finally destroyed after the Battle of Culloden. Today the Scalan is open all year round and visitors are welcome to visit and explore the site and see the original foundations, which are still visible near a small bridge.

The walk is fairly tame, but owing to the long hill climb it has its tiring moments so be warned. The trail starts out form the Eskemulloch car park and rambles along a flat path past the Scalan site. Passing by the site the trail heads up to some ruins at the Clash of Scalan, after which the path turns sharply right and travels steadily uphill to the summit of Tom Trumper, passing some grouse butts where some members of the elite stand in holes and sportingly blast unarmed birds to their ancient rallying call of "Good shot old bean!" However, once you've reached the cairn at the top and have spent enough time taking in the views, you head back down the hill following your tracks for a short while, until you pick up the return markers along a different route from outward trail: check the map, because the path is very faint!

Brown Hare

Braes of Glenlivet Heritage Trail
Walk 2 (6.6km, 4 miles)

Please note, at certain times the walk may be subject to deer stalking activities in the evenings and early mornings. The walk also passes through fields with livestock, leaving it unwise to let the dog off the lead.

Location: The car park is located at the end of the Chapeltown road, 7 miles from Tomintoul.

Extras

 Free parking is available at the start of the walk reached off the single track access road a few hundred metres past the Braecal Distillery.

 The nearest public toilets are in Tomintoul 7 miles south.

 Nearest:
Accommodation - B&B's, hotels guests houses and self-catering in and around Tomintoul 7 miles form the walks start.
Food - Around Tomintoul, 7 miles.
Fuel Station - Grantown-on-Spey 21 miles from the walks start.

G

Bochel Circuit

Glenlivet / Tomintoul

see walk diagram on map page 198

Walk Data

Orientation
Circuit route

Length
6.2 miles (10 km)

Grade
● Moderate

Time
2½ hours

Height Gain
90m (295ft)

Hills & Steeps
Gental gradients

Terrain
Natural & road

Markings
Walk number 10

Wheelchairs
No access

Access for Prams
Not suitable

Key Features

Woods & water trail with varied wildlife

Good View points

Crombie Waters

Noise Indicator

Natural sounds plus the odd vehicle.

Start from Tombae Quarry Car Park

Although this is rated an easy walk - and it is - it's still over 6 miles long and some stamina is required if you wish to make it to the end without extra oxygen. You will also need some idea of basic navigation, as some of the marker posts can be confusing.

However, this is a fine low-level walk along different surfaces via varying elements including a walk along a stretch of water, to a trail across open moorland and a section through pine trees. At no time does the walk become demanding with steep hills, although there are some steepish gradients. You also get to share the walk with lots of farm animals such as bulls - indeed, there is a notice of what to do if cows approach you near a gate-post (frankly if the Sunday lunch does make a bee-line for you, just shout the words 'rare, medium or well done' and the creature will soon get the message and beat a hasty retreat).

The walk starts from the Tombae Quarry car park, which is found on the road running behind the Tamnavulin Distillery. From the car park you set off along a short stretch of road until you are directed down a path which leads to a series of three bridges and a stretch of farmland with animals. After crossing all three bridges (one road and two foot) you are presented with a signpost arrowing straight on or right. It makes no odds which way you go as this is the start of the circuit, so you will end up back at this point.

Make my day, blister and climb the fence!!!!!

Bochel Circuit
Walk 10 (10km, 6.2miles)

Go straight ahead and you walk up a hill and turn right along a path that leads into a moorland. You follow the walk that takes you around a hill to your right and after walking through a wood you will come to a main road: here you walk down the tarmac for a hundred meters past a cottage and then return to the natural path as directed to on the right. Eventually you will reach the point where you had a choice of which way to go - from this point retrace the route back to the start.

 Far too much livestock to let the dog off the lead.

Location: Access the car park from the north of Tomnavoulin.

Extras

 Free parking is available at the start of the walk reached off the single track access road behind the Tomnavoulin Distillery.

 The nearest public toilets are in Tomintoul 7½ miles south.

Nearest:
 Accommodation - Minmore House in Glenlivet (4 miles) and the Croft Inn north of Auchbreck (3 miles). Food - Tomnavoulin General Store, 500 meters and Croft Inn, 2 miles. Fuel Station - Grantwon-on-Spey 21½ miles south west.

G

Clash Wood

Glenlivet / Tomintoul see walk diagram on map page 198

Walk Data

Orientation
Circuit route

Length
2 miles (3.2 km)

Grade
● Easy

Time
1 hour

Height Gain
150m (492ft)

Hills & Steeps
Gradual gradient

Terrain
Vehicle track

Markings
Walk Route 9

Wheelchairs
No access

Access for Prams
Passible

Key Features

Woodland trail with
varied wildlife

Good View points

Cycling Routes

Noise Indicator

Lots of bird song,
plus the odd vehicle.

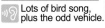
Start from the West Wood Car Park

The name of this simple walk has nothing to do with the 80's pop/punk band The Clash, the name simply relates to the woods; so don't expect squirrels with pins in their noses wearing ripped jeans to pop out and do a rendition of 'London Calling'. However, despite this not being a music trail, it is a good family walk that will take no more than an hour to complete and you simply can't go wrong, there's no need for sat nav's or maps, this walk is simplicity itself - a child of two could do it while sucking on its dummy and juggling Lego as it goes.

The wood lies close to Tomnavoulin with the walk following a hard vehicle track through a thick forest and along farmland. The route also forms one Glenlivet's many cycle trails. You start off a short road between Tomnavoulin and the Glenlivet distillery (sometimes smelling the heady mash in the air).

From the car park you follow the number 9 walk as shown on the signposts. Head up the track into the trees and after a short distance you will come to a junction. Ignoring the sign on the left, bear right and continue straight ahead along the track which is wide and hard-based and travels up hill with a gradual incline. After a short while the walk opens out on the left to reveal stunning views with farm-land running along side the path. About half a mile on you come to another junction at which point you turn right and continue following the route 9 markers which take you back into the woods with trees once again lining the trail. After passing through a couple of gates, you join up with the outward trail and turn left to return to the start.

Please note, in mid-late summer the walk may be subject to deer stalking activities in the evenings and early mornings.

 Good free-running walk for dogs with no restrictions, but livestock are in neighbouring fields.

Location: Heading north out of Tomnavoulin, take the road on the left as sign posted with a walk sign and 500meters on is the car park.

Jackdaw

Extras

 Free parking is available at the start of the walk reached off the single track access road between Tomnavoulin and the Glenlivet Distillery.

 The nearest public toilets are in Tomintoul 7 miles south.

Nearest:
Accommodation - Minmore House in Glenlivet (3 miles) and the Croft Inn north of Auchbreck (2 miles).
Food - Tomnavoulin General Store, 500 meters and Croft Inn, 2 miles.
Fuel Station - Grantown-on-Spey 21 miles south west.

G

Drumin Circular & Castle Walk

Glenlivet / Tomintoul

see walk diagram on map page 208

Walk Data

Orientation
Circuit route

Length
2 miles (3.2 km)

Grade
● Easy

Time
1½ hours

Height Gain
Minimal

Hills & Steeps
One short steep

Terrain
Natural paths

Markings
Drumin Circular

Wheelchairs
No access

Access for Prams
Possible

Key Features

Wood & water trail
with varied wildlife

Good View points

Historic Building

River Livet

Noise Indicator

Bird song mixed
with water and cars.

Walk starts from the castle car park

Looking for a family orientated easy walk with varying features and a large dollop of history? Well look no further, because the Drumin Circular is one of the nicest in the Cairngorms National Park.

It starts at the car park below the castle ruins and heads along a stretch of the River Livet, which at one point it traverses via a suspension bridge constructed by the Royal Engineers back in July 2000.

The first part of the walk involves passing through a number of small gates, which are in place to allow livestock to reach the river in order to drink. After passing the river you are taken up to a main road, which you cross, to head right for the track to the Glenlivet Distillery. A few yards on you cross over another road and enter a gate onto a path which leads into a wood. You follow the signs straight down the woods, which come out near the Glenlivet Medical Centre, opposite the slip road down to the castle car park, your access to the castle via a hill-path.

After climbing the steps to the castle you can choose to view the ruins via the gardens or from the rear of the castle. The exact history of Drumin Castle, a fortified tower house dating from the 15th century, is sketchy, with few historical documents available, but it's said that King Robert II granted the lands of Strathdon, including Drumin, to his son Alexander Stewart (better known as the "Wolf of Badenoch") in 1372. Today the castle is just a ruin with only one wall remaining. The 500-metre walk up only takes a few minutes but it is steep however, and there is an alternative disabled access. Check out the amazing tall and varied trees near the steps.

Drumin Circular Walk

Extras

 Free parking is available at the start of the walk in the car park at the base of the castle. There is also a separate upper car park for disabled visitors.

 For dog walkers: there is livestock around and you do have to cross roads. But there are sections where the dog can run.

Location: Drumin Castle is located in Glenlivet off the B9136, 11 miles from Tomintoul.

 The nearest public toilets are in Tomintoul 11 miles away.

Nearest:
Accommodation - Minmore House in Glenlivet and various B&B's, hotels, self-catering and hotels in Tomintoul 11 miles away.
Food - Tomnavoulin General Store, 3 mlies, and Croft Inn, 3 miles.
Fuel Station - Grantwon-on-Spey 19 miles south west.

G

Glen Brown - Kylnadrochit

Glenlivet / Tomintoul   see walk diagram on map page 199

Walk Data

Orientation
Circuit route

Length
4 miles (6.3 km)

Grade
● Moderate

Time
1½ hours

Height Gain
90m (197ft)

Hills & Steeps
Long hill

Terrain
Vehicle tracks

Markings
Walk number 8

Wheelchairs
No access

Access for Prams
Not suitable

Key Features

Wood & moors trail with varied wildlife

Good View points

Burn of Brown

Noise Indicator

Some vehicle noise plus lots of bird song.

Walk starts from White Bridge Car Park

The Glen Brown walk is a low-level, no-nonsense trail taking you through a lot of farmland via a thick pine wood in an area just off the A939 between Tomintoul and Grantown-on-Spey.

The walk is set out on the Glenlivet Estate (a Crown Estate) and what is immediately evident is just how well it's managed. The route is set out across a stretch of land that will take you across farmland, over moorland and through a thick wood. But: although the route is marked out, the path often disappears and some marker posts are either missing or not clear.

The trail is rated as moderate, but this is not a hard walk. That said, the route does rise to above 400 metres, and at 4 miles long with some long hill stretches, it's not a walk for the casual 10-a-day burger freak.

210

The walk starts from the White Bridge car park, a quarter of a mile up the road from the Bridge of Brown along the A939. Following the route number 8 marker posts, you head uphill along a forest. The route soon crosses into fields with livestock and snakes along an uneven and often very soft track. Having cleared the initial fields you are led into a thick wood walking close by Kylnadrochit Lodge. After 15 minutes you pass through a high gate and head round the trees to meet up eventually with a hill moorland section which will take you westwards and alongside the Burn of Brown, until the trail meets up with the A939 access road near the Bridge of Brown, where there is a cafe located on a bend in the hill. At the road you turn right and walk back up the tarmac to the start point at the White Bridge car park.

Please note, between June and July the walk may be subject to deer stalking activities in the evenings and early mornings.

Sections of the walk have farm animals so take extra care - keep Rover on the lead.

Location: The White Bridge car park is 5 miles from Tomintoul along the A939.

sparrowhawk

Walk · 8

Extras

 Free parking is available at the White Bridge car park of the A939

The nearest public toilets are in Tomintoul 5 miles away.

Nearest:
Accommodation - B&B's, hotels guests houses and self-catering in and around Tomintoul 5 miles form the walks start at White Bridge.
Food - Bridge of Brown Cafe 1/4 of a mile from the start of the walk.
Fuel Station - Grantown-on-Spey 9.5 miles from the walk's start.

G

211

Glenconglass to Carn Daimh

Glenlivet / Tomintoul see walk diagram on map page 200

Walk Data

Orientation
Circuit route

Length
7.3 miles (11.8 km)

Grade
● Challenging

Time
3 hours

Height Gain
240m (787ft)

Hills & Steeps
High and steep

Terrain
Natural & vehicle

Markings
Walk number 6

Wheelchairs
No access

Access for Prams
Not suitable

Key Features

Wood & moors trail with varied wildlife

Good View points

Cycling Routes

Noise Indicator

Very quiet walk with only natural sounds.

Start from the Glenconglass Car Park

Some walks are not for everyone, and this is one of them: it will have you sweating, especially by the time you get to summit of Carn Daimh at 570m (1,870 feet).

The path is located 3 miles north of Tomintoul of the B9136, and if you don't like long hill walks - much of this one is up a wide vehicle trek through a wild forest - then stay at home and tune into the Trisha show, as that will be far less stressful on the body.

It's not just good footwear you need here: you will need a heart in good working order, a good head for heights and a clean pair of lungs untarnished by cigarettes, because for the first hour and a half it's uphill, and although the first part is fairly sedate, it gets tougher as you go higher and deeper into the woods, which in places have suffered some severe storm damage, fallen trees in evidence.

From the Glenconglass car park follow the walk number 6 and head along the wide vehicle track towards the woods, which are just ahead. Part of the trail is a cycle route: none of it has any scary obstacles to scale, but it's soon evident that you are in for a long haul and as you enter the woods the trail seems to go on and on. En-route you pass a couple of height markers which only seem to prolong the agony and the summit arrival. However, once you do clear the woods, the top soon comes in to view and from here, after savouring the view and downing a gallon of Lucozade Sport, you head back down the hill, which will now take you over a heather moorland which is very soft and boggy in places. Eventually the path comes out at a small burn - simply cross the small bridge and head through the farm to the start.

Please note, between June and July the walk may be subject to deer stalking activities in the evenings and early mornings.

 Provided the dog is up to it, this is an excellent walk.

Location: Glenconglass car park is 3 miles north of Tomintoul along B9136 and is well sign posted.

Small White

Carn Daimh
Walk 6
(12km, 7.3miles)

Extras

 Free parking in the Glenconglass car park off the B9136.

 The nearest public toilets are in Tomintoul 3 miles away.

 Nearest:
Accommodation - B&B's, hotels guests houses and self-catering in and around Tomintoul 3 miles form the walks start at Glenconglass .
Food - Around Tomintoul, 3 miles.
Fuel Station - Grantown-on-Spey 17 miles from the start.

G

Glenmulliach Forest Nature Trail

Glenlivet / Tomintoul   see walk diagram on map page 200

Walk Data

Orientation
Circuit route

Length
3 miles (4.8 km)

Grade
● Easy

Time
1½ hours

Height Gain
90m (295ft)

Hills & Steeps
Steep introduction

Terrain
Natural paths

Markings
Nature Trail sign

Wheelchairs
No access

Access for Prams
Not suitable

Key Features

Woodland trail with varied wildlife

Good View points

Forest Nature Trail

Picnic site

Noise Indicator

Wildlife sounds plus vehicles passing by.

Start from the car park just off the A939

Glenmulliach Forest is located three miles west of Tomintoul of the A939 road which passes through the Lecht snow grounds a few miles away. The nature walk is a really nice family spot kids will love and adults will also enjoy, as it's basic and easy, although there is a steep section at the beginning of the trail.

The walk is set out around a small wood which aims to inform the visitor about the wildlife and nature that can be found in the area, and as you walk through the tight trees you are presented with helpful information plaques giving you details on the animals, insects, trees and plants of the area. The plaques give details on red squirrels, moles, roe deer, buzzards and even black slugs. You can also read about larch trees, rowan trees and different fungi such as fly agaric. All the plaques are placed in convenient spots and are easy to read and very child friendly.

The walk begins from the car park, which also doubles up as a picnic site with a small water feature. After a few minutes the trail heads uphill, and if you have sluggish children or moaning ones, then it's in this section that they will play up. However, the woods are full of interesting features and the steep part doesn't last for too long. The walk can be done in two sections, a short woodland trail or a longer hike to a forest hide and further still to a view point, either way both are tame trails on uneven surfaces which won't suit a pram. The marker posts are well placed so you will be able to get round with ease, and if you choose to visit the hide or view point, you do so returning along the same path. The final stretch of the walk back to the car park takes you through an eerily dark part of woods with a carpet of pine needles on the ground, making it a very interesting spot.

Please note, between June and July the walk may be subject to deer stalking activities in the evenings and early mornings.

 The walk is fine for letting the dog off the lead.

Location: The walk is of the A939, 3 miles east of Tomintoul.

Red Squirrel

Extras

 Free parking in the picnic site car park of the A939 snow resort road.

 The nearest public toilets are in Tomintoul 3 miles away.

Nearest:
Accommodation - B&B's, hotels guests houses and self-catering in and around Tomintoul 3 miles form the walks start at Glenconglass .
Food - Around Tomintoul, 3 miles.
Fuel Station - Grantown-on-Spey 17 miles from the start.

G

Knock Earth House - West Avonside

Glenlivet / Tomintoul see walk diagram on map page 200

Walk Data

Orientation
Point to Point

Length (Return)
5.3 miles (8.5km)

Grade
● Easy

Time (Return)
2½ hours

Height Gain
Minimal

Hills & Steeps
Flat low level

Terrain
Vehicle tracks

Markings
Walk number 11

Wheelchairs
No access

Access for Prams
Passible in parts

Key Features

Wood & water trail with varied wildlife

Good View points

River Avon

Noise Indicator

Noise comes form passing vehicles.

Start from the Balcorach Car Park

This is a walk is in two parts, one a straight point-to-point riversider along the Avon - a round trip of 4 miles - the other a side walk to the Knock Earth House, a protected ancient monument, adding about a mile and a quarter to the journey.

The Knock Earth House dates back to late Bronze Age of 1200 BC and it's thought the place was initially used as a souterrain. The word souterrain comes from French 'sous terrain', which literally means 'under ground'. These ancient underground chambers or galleries would have been lined with either wood or stone, and were used to store food for their local settlements. The chamber existing today is also thought to have been used as an illicit whisky still, but all that's left is a stone-lined hole in the ground, ring-fenced to protect the site which you can get close to and view.

The walk starts from the Balcorach car park half a mile from the Tomintoul Distillery. From the notice board, you walk along the vehicle track for about half a mile until you come to a sign directing you to turn left to the site, which is about half a mile up the track past an old farm. You will find the Knock Earth house on a small hill close to a house with a tower.

To continue doing the West Avonside walk you trace your steps back to the junction where you turned left, and simply turn left and follow the riverside number 11 walk. Eventually the trail winds through a small copse before dropping down towards the riverside, where you will come up to a suspension bridge built by the Royal Engineers in 2001. From here you can either walk back to the start point along the river path, or cross over the bridge and walk up to the B9136 road. At the top turn right and walk along the tarmac to the original start point, taking care to look out for on coming vehicles.

 Farm animals are present for most of the walk, so keep the dog under full control.

Location: Balcorach car park is 9 miles north of Tomintoul.

Collared Dove

West Avonside Path (Walk 11) To Altnaglander (3.5km, 2miles)

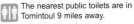

Extras

Free parking in the Balcorach car park off the B9136.

The nearest public toilets are in Tomintoul 9 miles away.

Nearest:
Accommodation - B&B's, hotels guests houses and self-catering in and around Tomintoul 9 miles form the walks start at Balcorach.
Food - Around Tomintoul, 9 miles.
Fuel Station - Grantown-on-Spey 18 miles from the start.

G

217

Tom Dubh Wood Walk

Glenlivet / Tomintoul see walk diagram on map page 201

Walk Data

Orientation
Circuit route

Length
1.5 miles (2.5km)

Grade
• Easy

Time
45 minutes

Height Gain
68m (223ft)

Hills & Steeps
Gentle rise

Terrain
Natural path

Markings
Walk number 7

Wheelchairs
No access

Access for Prams
Possible but soft

Key Features

Woodland trail with varied wildlife

Good View points

Whisky Distillery

Noise Indicator

Quiet walk with bird song and the odd car

Start from the road opposite the Croft Inn

There are simple walks and there are simple walks, and they don't get more simple than the Tom Dubh Wood, which sits overlooking the Glenlivet Whisky Distillery - if the wind is blowing in the right direction you can smell the aroma of the malted barley as it wafts across the fields and through the pine trees which surround the woods on all sides.

The Glenlivet Distillery, which is visible through an opening in the trees, is the oldest legal distillery in Scotland, which began life back in 1824 courtesy of George Smith and his youngest son. The site in Glenlivet was chosen for a number of important reasons, most fundamentally the superb quality of the spring water found in the local rivers and burns. Today the distillery produces single malt Scotch whisky using copper stills and oak casks unchanged since the business was established.

Head down the B9009 Dufftown road and opposite the Croft Inn is a road. A short distance down you will see a sign pointing to the start of the walk. Pass through the gate and then walk up the hill to the woods, which lay 500 metres ahead. Passing through another gate, you enter the woods, which are very thick and dark in places - sometimes natural light can barely penetrate to the forest floor.

This place was peaceful until you showed up

You can do this walk clockwise or anticlockwise, it makes no difference as the path simply travels around the woods along a wide soft vehicle track, both pleasant and easy to complete. At one point there is a clearing to reveal the Glenlivet Distillery across a field less than a mile away. The walk will take about 45 minutes and apart from the sound of occasional vehicles travelling along nearby roads, this is a quiet walk with numerous birds chirping away en-route.

Extras

 There is no car park at the start of the walk, the nearest is at the Croft in 200 metres away. However, you will need to ask for permission or be a customer.

 Toilets are available to customers of the Croft Inn. The nearest public toilets are in Tomintoul, 11 miles.

 The walk is fenced in from nearby farmland with livestock, making this a good free run with a dog off the lead.

G

Location: The path is located of the B9009 opposite the Croft Inn.

Nearest:
Accommodation - Croft Inn or Minmore House in Glenlivet, also various B&B's, hotels, self-catering and hotels in Tomintoul, 11 miles.
Food - Croft Inn or Tomnavoulin General Store, 3 mlies away.
Fuel Station - Grantown-on-Spey 19 miles south west.

Tomnavoulin - Carn Daimh Circuit

Glenlivet / Tomintoul see walk diagram on map page 201

Walk Data

Orientation
Circuit route

Length
5 miles (8 km)

Grade
● moderate

Time
2½ hours

Height Gain
310m (1017ft)

Hills & Steeps
Steep hill

Terrain
Natural & vehicle

Markings
Walk number 5

Wheelchairs
No access

Access for Prams
Not suitable

Key Features

Wood & moors trail with varied wildlife

Good View points

Cycling Routes

Noise Indicator

Natural sounds free of vehicles noise.

Start from the West Wood Car Park

The walk over the summit of Carn Daimh, starting out near the hamlet of Tomnavoulin, is a walk holding no great surprises, but it'll get the old ticker pumping away since it takes you up to a summit which serves as a look-out for golden plovers, who cry to each other 570m (1,870 feet) above sea level.

There are no oxygen cylinders or drink stations en-route, so don't do this one if you're the sort of person who breaks out in a sweat just going to the bar to get the drinks in.

That aside, if you are healthy then no worries, because although the route takes you high up, the trail is along a good path and at no time does the trek require you to strap on crampons or pull out an ice axe - nor do you have to scale any obstacles. This is a moderate walk because of its length and the fact that the first 90 minutes is all uphill.

The walk starts from the car park at Clash Wood, where you follow the route 5 sign up the vehicle trail. After about four hundred metres you turn left of the track and drop down along a narrow path which takes you through the woods to a farmland section. You walk for some time along tracks that take you through, or via farmland until you reach the woods on Carn Ellick, which lead on to the summit of Carn Ellick. On the way the route is well marked, so no great navigation skills are needed, but it's always a good idea to check a map for long hill walks.

Golden Plover

Along the way you pass over different terrain surfaces from vehicle tracks to moorland paths, which in places can be very wet and boggy. But overall the paths are flat and easy to walk along, with no rocks and roots to trip you up. Eventually the track joins up with the Clash Wood walk 9 route that takes you back to the start point.

Walk 5

Extras

 Free parking is available at the start of the walk reached of the single track access road between Tomnavoulin and the Glenlivet Distillery.

 The nearest public toilets are in Tomintoul 7 miles south.

Farm animals are present for most of the time, so keep the dog under full control.

Location: Heading north out of Tomnavoulin, take the road on the left as sign posted with a walk sign and 500meters on is the car park.

Nearest:
Accommodation - Minmore House in Glenlivet (3 miles) and the Croft Inn north of Auchbreck (2 miles). Food - Tomnavoulin General Store, 500 meters and Croft Inn, 2 miles. Fuel Station - Grantown-on-Spey 21 miles south west.

G

Ben Newe Forest Walks

Walk Data

 Orientation
Circuit routes

 Length
600m to 2¼ miles

 Grade
● Easy

 Time
15 mins to 2 hours

 Height Gain
180m (590ft)

 Hills & Steeps
Steep hill

 Terrain
Natural & vehicle

 Markings
Colour arrows

 Wheelchairs
No access

 Access for Prams
Not suitable

Key Features

 Woodland trail with varied wildlife

 Good View point

 Picnic site

Noise Indicator

 Forest sounds plus the vehicle noise.

Walks start from the car park just off the A97

Four miles east of Strathdon lies this low-key unassuming woodland site, which has a set of short and fun family trails with a picnic site.

The woods are set back a few hundred metres off the A97 route in the direction of Alford and Aberdeen, and what you will find here is three short walks which, although similar in terms of terrain and features, are however different in the lengths and gradients they negotiate.

The longest is the yellow trail, which may take you by surprise, travelling up a long and often steep hill, through a section of tall and tight pine trees. Indeed, at one point the trees hang low and almost swallow up the path at the north and top steep section. Like all the walks, you follow the yellow arrow from the car park and immediately you head uphill. It's not until you have walked for at least 30 minutes that the walk begins to taper out and head downhill again. The trail moves along a wide path that is relatively flat and free of any obstacles. Along the walk there are openings through the trees with long views across Strathdon and Glenbuchat, where you will find the ruins of Glenbuchat Castle. The total walk time for the yellow trails is around 1 hour from start to finish.

Common Shrew

The green trail, which initially follows part of the yellow walk, is much smaller, and rather than going all the way up to the top of the woods it travels around a lower section of the forest. With a total walk time of about 30 minutes, this is a good family trail.

The shortest is the red route, which in many ways is hardly a walk at all, and if it wasn't for the marker posts sticking out through the long vegetation, it would be impossible to follow the trail at all as the path is non-existent.

Extras

 Free parking is available at the start of the walk just off the A97.

 There are no convenient public toilets near the walk, the nearest town with facilities is at Alford, 16 miles away

This is a good wood for walking a dog off the lead and apart from the access road there are no worries, such as livestock.

Nearest:
Accommodation - In and around Strathdon there are a couple of hotels and B&Bs 4 miles from the walk site. Alford has a greater selection and is 16 miles away.
Food - Strathdon Stores for snacks, Alford for restaurants/cafes.
Fuel Station - Alford 16 miles away.

Location: The car park is located 4 miles from Strathdon off the A97.

S

Kincraig-*Glenfeshie* & Kingussie

In the west of the Cairngorms National Park and south of Aviemore are the village of Kincraig and the town of Kingussie, both of which lie along the banks of the River Spey.

The walks that you can do in this area vary enormously, from waymarked town-orientated routes in Kingussie to stunningly remote family walks in Glenfeshie near Kincraig.

The walks associated with the Uath Lochans in Glenfeshie are absolutely stunning and the lochan trail is possibly the finest short family stroll in Scotland. It is utterly glorious.

A first for the Cairngorms National Park is the Sculpture Trail at Feshiebridge in Kincraig, a short and very interesting walk with unusual images carved out of trees and stone whose enigmatic stories may well have you scratching your head in wonder...

Walk with history, checking out the short trail from Kingussie to Ruthven Barracks - an ancient monument dating back to 1229. Birdwatchers will be in their elements at the Insh Marshes Nature Reserve, run by the RSPB, where you are able to see, close up, many rare wading and water birds.

Ki

Ku

Farleitter Crag & Ridge Walk (see page 230)

Kincraig Speyside & Woods Walk (see page 234)

River Feshie and Sculpture Trail (see page 236)

Feshiebridge Woodland Walk (see page 232)

Loch Insh Interpretative Trail (see page 238)

For full size maps: www.cairngormslivingwalks.com

The Duke of Gordon's Monument Walk (see page 240)

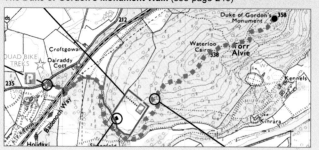

Uath Lochans to Feshiebridge
(see page 244)

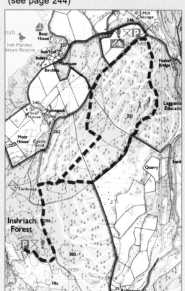

Uath Lochans (see page 242)

Ki
Ku

Birch Woodie (The Hazel Woods)
(see page 246)

Insh Marshes - Invertromie Trail (see page 50)

Creag Bheag Trail (see page 248)

Jubilee Walk to Ruthven Barracks
(see page 252)

Kingussie Golf Course Circular
(see page 254)

Tom Baraidh Walk(see page 258

Ruthven Barracks & Glen Tromie (see page 256)

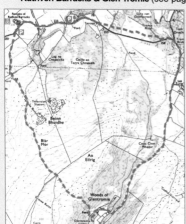

West Terrace Circular
(see page 260)

Farleitter Crag & Ridge Walk

Kincraig - Glenfeshie see walk diagram on map page 226

Walk Data

Orientation
Circuit route

Length
2.2 miles (3.5km)

Grade
● Moderate

Time
1½ hours

Height Gain
50m (164ft)

Hills & Steeps
Steep

Terrain
Natural paths

Markings
▶▶ Red & green

Wheelchairs
No access

Access for Prams
Not suitable

Key Features

Woodland trail with varied wildlife

Good View points

Steep Rock Face

Uath Lochans

Noise Indicator

Various forest sounds.

Start the walk from the lochans car park

In the Inshriach Forest near Glenfeshie are two superb high-level walks which take you through 120-year-old Scots pines up to a viewpoint with stunning vistas.

The Farleitter Crag and Farleitter Ridge walks are marked out as two separate tracks on the information board posted in the car park, but you could do them as one. The Ridge route (green) is 1.2 miles long and follows the Crag for the first part, taking in the steep trail up to the top of the Crag, but then it takes a short cut back down to the start point: nevertheless it's a good wee trek, and a tester on the legs (and it's not for those who can't handle heights).

The Farleitter Crag is a great walk high up to a stunning viewpoint, before descending through a thick pine wood – its path is good, but steep in parts.

You begin both walks from the car park at Uath Lochans in a westward direction along a wide path. After a short distance you come to a junction where you bear right along the red and green route. Soon afterwards you begin to go up hill and it's not long before you realise how high the trail is - in parts you will actually find yourself leaning into the hill. After a while you'll find yourself walking along the top of the steep crag (N.B. if you step over the edge at this point, your lights will go out for ever, so take care!!)

Common Shrew

The path eventually levels out, all the while travelling through trees until you come to a couple of view-points with benches. After catching your breath you can head back into the forest following a trail that winds its way back to the start.

Inshriach Forest is part of an ancient Caledonian pinewood and is home to all sorts of wildlife.

 For dog walkers, the one area to beware of is along the top of the crag, as there is a steep drop, so keep Pluto close until you get back into the woods.

Location: Take the access road off the B970 left of Insh House.

Extras

Free parking is available at the start of the walk.

 No public toilets, the nearest are at the Loch Insh centre, 1-1/2 miles away. Patrons only

Nearest:
Accommodation - All Kincraig.
Ossian Hotel (01540) 651 242.
Loch Insh Centre 01540 651 272
visit - www.visitkincraig.com
Food - Ossian Hotel (01540) 651 242.
Loch Insh Centre 01540 651 272
Fuel Station - Aviemore 7 miles.

Contact for further details:
www.forestry.gov.uk

Ki
Ku

231

Feshiebridge Woodland Walk

Kincraig see walk diagram on map page 226

Walk Data

 Orientation
Circuit route

 Length
3 miles (1.9 km)

 Grade
● Easy

 Time
1 hour

 Height Gain
50m (164ft)

 Hills & Steeps
Long hill

 Terrain
Natural paths

 Markings
▶ Yellow marker

 Wheelchairs
No access

 Access for Prams
Not suitable

Key Features

 Wood & river trail
with varied wildlife

 Varied Wildlife

 River Feshie

Noise Indicator

Forest noise mixed
with water rush.

Start the walk from Feshiebridge

The Feshiebridge Woodland walk is a plain and simple family affair along a route that runs close the River Feshie. It starts next to a spot popular with locals in the summer months, when dare-devils can be seen jumping off the bridge into the pool below: the bridge spans the Feshie at spot where the water cascades over rocks towards the point a mile ahead where it joins the River Spey.

The walk starts from the car park a few hundred metres up from the bridge. Following the yellow posts, you walk along to the bridge, but rather than going under you have to go up and over via a gate. On the other side of the road, and staying on the same side, you come to a number of houses and a clearing which will give access to the downward path to the water for a picture, but note - you have to cut through some thick and rough vegetation, which is steep in places.

Passing the house on your right, you continue along the yellow marked route with no obstacles. Eventually you will come to a stone wall with a large metal gate - at this point, rather than passing through you turn right at the marker and follow a much thinner path uphill along the wall. As the path levels out it veers away from the wall and heads for the tall pine trees. A short way in you come to a junction: here you turn right and walk down the path until you come to Balcraggan B&B, at which point you turn right to the road. Turning right, you walk down the tarmac for 50 metres until you see the car park sign on the left, where you simply follow the signs.

Orange-tip Buterfly

With trout and salmon sometimes plentiful in the clear waters of the Feshie, you may well see an osprey fishing, and deer often drink at the water's edge. In the woods you may encounter a red or hear a weasel scurrying around.

It's a good walk all the way with your dog off the lead, but keep it near you at the bridge because of the fast- flowing water.

Location: The car park at the start of the bridge is a few hundred metres along from Feshiebridge.

Extras

 Free parking is available at the start of the walk.

 No public toilets, the nearest conviencies are at the Loch Insh centre, 1-1/2 miles away. Patrons only

 Nearest:
Accommodation - All Kincraig.
Ossian Hotel (01540) 651 242.
Loch Insh Centre 01540 651 272
visit - www.visitkincraig.com
Loch Insh Centre (01540) 651 272
Food - Ossian Hotel (01540) 651 242.
Loch Insh Centre 01540 651 272
Fuel Station - Aviemore 7 miles.

 Contact for further details:
www.forestry.gov.uk

Ki
Ku

233

Kincraig Speyside & Woods Walk

Kincraig

see walk diagram on map page 226

Walk Data

Orientation
Circuit route

Length
1.2 miles (2 km)

Grade
● Easy

Time
25 minutes

Height Gain
Minimal

Hills & Steeps
A steep hill

Terrain
Tarmac & natural

Markings
None

Wheelchairs
No access

Access for Prams
Not suitable

Key Features

Wood & loch trail with varied wildlife

Good View points

Loch Insh

Noise Indicator

Woodland sounds with the odd car.

Start the walk opposite Ossian Hotel

Kincraig is one of the nicest villages in Speyside, with its quaint village shop, mountain views and the stunning Loch Insh.

There are lots of small walks that you can simply do on your own without any way-markers. You can walk through wooded areas using the paths eked out over many years .

Walking from the top of the village, opposite the Ossian Hotel, head along Dunachton Road and at the first junction turn left and follow the road to its end where you will find a step down to a path sandwiched between a house called Birkhill and Skeravoe. Walk along the narrow path until it comes out at a driveway. Go straight ahead and after 25 metres you will see, on your right, a gate leading into a birch wood. Pass through and head left: after a minute or two you come to a gate in a fence by the railway line.

Cross over the railway and enter a field with a spectacular view of the Cairngorms. Here you can choose to turn left and follow a path down a steep hill which leads to a gate near the village shop, passing a ruined cottage on route. Alternatively, you can go straight ahead and follow the path towards the loch. This route will also bring you out at the gate near the village shop after a pleasant waterside stroll. Either way there are no way-markers, but you won't get lost if you keep your eyes open.

Being so close to Insh Marshes and with its own island, Kincraig is host to lots of different birds, with species changing over the year. Look out for geese, swans, herons, oyster-catchers, sand martins, ospreys (I could go on). Birds apart, there are otters in the area (but you have to be very lucky – perhaps about dusk between the island and the bridge).

Otter

Extras

There are no car parks at the start of the walk.

There are no public toilets in Kincraig.

Nearest:
Accommodation - All Kincraig.
Ossian Hotel (01540) 651 242.
Loch Insh Centre 01540 651 272
visit - www.visitkincraig.com.
Food - Ossian Hotel (01540) 651 242.
Fuel Station - Aviemore 7 miles.

Walking the dog off the lead is fine, but note the open areas around the loch often have sheep and lambs grazing – have a look before going through the gate!

Location: Kincraig lies six miles south of Aviemore. Dunachton Road is opposite the Ossian Hotel.

Ki
Ku

River Feshie and Sculpture Trail

Walk Data

Orientation
Circuit route

Length
1.2 miles (2km)

Grade
● Easy

Time
45 minutes

Height Gain
Minimal

Hills & Steeps
Small hill

Terrain
Natural

Markings
▶ Red marker

Wheelchairs
Sculpture Trail

Access for Prams
Sculpture Trail

Key Features

Wood & river trail with varied wildlife

Good View points

Picnic tables

River Feshire

Noise Indicator

Water rush and bird sounds.

Start the walk from Feshiebridge

The River Feshie is an important tributary of the River Spey. It flows from Glenfeshie and after descending four miles it joins the Spey at Kincraig.

The walk is a really simple one with no big hills to worry about - there is a small uphill section half-way round, but it's not testing and can be handled by anyone.

You begin the walk from the centre of the car park by picking up the red marker post and following the track down to the river. The path drops down and bears left along a track which can often be overgrown and is rough and uneven in many parts. You follow the line of the river, which actually splits and returns on itself, crossing over a number of small wooden bridges as you go. Being so close to the river, the path can often be flooded and may well be wet and muddy.

After about 10 minutes the path turns sharply left up a steep step with wooden runners. At the top you come to a walled garden with a gate which leads you into the Frank Bruce Sculpture Trail, an area set aside for the exhibition of some beautifully sculpted stone and wood structures which encapsulate both man's method and his madness.

Dragon Fly

The pieces punctuate a trail which starts off in an open garden ringed by a stone wall before descending into a dense wood. You simply follow the path and at each turn you come across another exhibit. All are clearly marked and named. Note: some of the images are quite intense, and young children may find them more disconcerting than diverting...

One World

The Sculpture Trail is not long and as it's on a good path, pushing a pram will pose no problems.

 There are no serious concerns for walking the dog off the lead around here, but remember the road is near the car park.

Location: The car park at the start of the bridge is a few hundred metres along from Feshiebridge.

Extras

 Free parking is available at the start of the walk.

 No public toilets, the nearest are at the Loch Insh centre, 1-1/2 miles away. Patrons only

Nearest:
Accommodation - All Kincraig.
Ossian Hotel (01540) 651 242.
Loch Insh Centre 01540 651 272
visit - www.visitkincraig.com
Food - Ossian Hotel (01540) 651 242.
Loch Insh Centre 01540 651 272
Fuel Station - Aviemore 7 miles.

 Contact for further details:
www.forestry.gov.uk

Ki

Ku

Loch Insh Interpretative Trail

Kincraig

see walk diagram on map page 226

Walk Data

 Orientation
Circuit route

 Length
1 mile

 Grade
• Easy

 Time
30 minutes

 Height Gain
Minimal

 Hills & Steeps
One steep

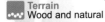 **Terrain**
Wood and natural

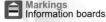 **Markings**
Information boards

Wheelchairs
No access

Access for Prams
Not suitable

Key Features

Loch side trail with varied wildlife

Watersports

Picnic Tables

Loch Insh

Noise Indicator

Natural sounds and people noise.

Start the walk from Loch Insh Boat House

Located at the Loch Insh Water Sports Centre in Kincraig, this is a fun trail set close to the water's edge. As well as being a learning walk with information boards, it's also an adventure tail with climbing frames, rope swings and other wooden obstacles to try out. There is also a "Kid's Kingdom" adventure play park.

Loch Insh is actually a widening of the River Spey and stretches between Kincraig and Insh with the RSPB marshes at the southern shores. The loch plays host to all sorts of watersports, from sailing to canoeing, windsurfing and kayaking. You can also take a wildlife boat tour, which will take you to parts of the loch not normally reachable.

A short distance out is a small island packed with wildlife and both the loch and island make a spectacular backdrop for a picture, especially in winter when the loch freezes.

The Interpretative Trail, which is free to visitors using the centre's facilities, is located at the end of the car park and travels along the waterside. The first part comprises a wooden path snaking around a small, stocked lagoon where novice anglers "cast" off, often for their very first time.

After a short stretch you turn left off the wooden path and walk uphill along a natural one, which winds its way through the trees, with one steep hill section in a dark area of the woods. Around the walk are a number of obstacle courses, which you can try out, but do take notice of the signs regarding safety and supervision. Also along the route are ten information boards, which give you details on the history of the area.

Kincraig can boast a huge variety of native wildlife, with deer, foxes, badgers and hares and numerous birds. It is also known that otters live near the loch, which osprey like to fish.

 This is not really a trail for walking the dog.

Location: The Loch Insh Watersports Centre is a mile from the village Post Office.

Spotted Crake

Extras

 There is free car park at the start of the walk for patrons.

 Toilets are available in the restaurant next to the car park, but for customers only.

Nearest:
Accommodation - All Kincraig. Ossian Hotel (01540) 651 242. Loch Insh Centre 01540 651 272
visit - www.visitkincraig.com
visit - www.visitkincraig.com
Food - Loch Insh Water Sports Centre. Ossian Hotel
Fuel Station - Aviemore 7 miles.

Ki

Ku

The Duke of Gordon's Monument Walk

Walk Data

Orientation
Point to Point

Length *(one way)*
2.4 miles (4 kms)

Grade
● Easy

Time *(one way)*
2 hours

Height Gain
138m (453ft)

Hills & Steeps
Gental steep

Terrain
Soft vehicle track

Markings
None

Wheelchairs
No access

Access for Prams
Not suitable

Key Features

Woodland trail with varied wildlife

Good View points

Monument

Noise Indicator

Lots of bird songs plus the odd car.

Start the walk next to Dalraddy Caravan site

This is a great walk, with stunning views, interesting fauna, lots of wildlife and history.

The walk takes you up Torr Alvie to a summit of 1100 metres (359m) and on which sits The Duke of Gordon's Monument, a 90ft column commemorating the 5th Duke and "Cock of the North" who died in 1836.

There are two ways to complete the walk: the wrong way and the right way... The wrong way would be to head straight up as the crow flies, because this is a steep hill and you will get seriously caught out in thick vegetation. However, there is an easy route via a well-worn vehicle track running up a ridge.

You gain access to the path through the Kinrara Estate at the Dalraddy Caravan Park. Only estate vehicles are allowed past the gates so walk down the tarmac road and over the railway line for about 5 minutes until you come to a section where the road bends to the right and is joined on the left by a track. Head left up the track and through the trees until you come to the bottom of a field. From here you are aiming to get to a gate, which is in the middle, and at the top of the field directly opposite an old shed. From the gate you will clearly see the vehicle tracks that will take you all the way to the top along a dirt track, which can be very muddy on a rainy day. The track runs out at the very top and it's only when you're close that you will see the monument.

Hen Pheasant

Overall this is an excellent and rewarding walk for the whole family, although not with a pram. From the top, the views are simply stunning and after savouring them for a few minutes or staying for a picnic, you simply trace your steps all the way back down.

This walk calls for good footwear.

 Because of pheasants and breeding grounds round the estate, dogs are not allowed.

Location: From Aviemore, the entrance via Dalraddy is 4 miles south along the B970.

Extras

 There is limited parking near the Dalraddy Caravan Park.

Nearest toilets are located at Dalraddy Caravan park, ask for permission though

Nearest:
Accommodation - Dalraddy Caravan Park just 5 metres away.
Food - In the caravan park there is a small shop where you can get refreshments.
Fuel Station - Aviemore, 4 miles.

Ki
Ku

Uath Lochans

Walk Data

Orientation
Circuit route

Length
1 mile

Grade
● Easy

Time
35 minutes

Height Gain
Minimal

Hills & Steeps
Short hill

Terrain
Earth and wood

Markings
▶ White marker

Wheelchairs
No access

Access for Prams
Not suitable

Key Features

Lochan & wood trail
with varied wildlife

Picnic Tables

Uath Lochans

Noise Indicator

Quiet walk with lots of bird songs.

Start the walk from the lochans car park

Think of any word which describes a natural beauty as spectacular, fantastic, wonderful and outstanding – it will certainly apply to Uath Lochans. Here we have, without doubt, one of the finest short walks in the whole of the Cairngorms National Park.

The Uath Lochans (pronounced by real locals as Oo-eth) are a collection of four small lochs located in the Inshriach Forest near Glenfeshie, managed by the Forestry Commission, and described in their own words as the strath's "best kept secret". It's absolutely true. But why this walk is not as popular as others in the highlands is a mystery. Mind you, given its tranquillity, it's probably a blessing that this is a secret gem.

All the same, this walk is far too good to be left to a select few and it will appeal to the whole family, from mum and dad, kids, granny and granddad right down to the cat, the dog and Harry the hamster - bring them all because they'll love it. It's quiet, remote, unspoilt, stunning.

To the left of the information board is the start of the walk, with its white marker post. Follow the path, which at times can be very soft and boggy. At times a wooden path takes over from the natural one and travels around and through the lochans. The trail is well laid out and you are greeted with all sorts of views and terrain features, from water pools, mountain views and pine woods to a high rock face. There are no hard parts in this walk, with one easy hill - but because of some soft parts, this is not a walk with a pram.

Around the walk you may well spot a buzzard and numerous water birds, but you will also notice just how many colour variations there are in the plants, trees and grass.

 There are no concerns for dog walkers. Let them run.

Location: Access to the Lochans is easy, along a tarmac road towards Glenfeshie. A mile after the turn-off from the B970 is a right turn for Uath Lochans.

Common Frog

Extras

 Free parking is available at the start of the walk.

 No public toilets, the nearest conviencies are at the Loch Insh centre, 1-1/2 miles away. Patrons only

 Nearest:
Accommodation - All Kincraig.
Ossian Hotel (01540) 651 242.
Loch Insh Centre 01540 651 272
visit - www.visitkincraig.com
Loch Insh Centre 01540 651 272
Food - Ossian Hotel (01540) 651 242.
Loch Insh Centre 01540 651 272
Fuel Station - Aviemore 7 miles.

 Contact for further details:
www.forestry.gov.uk

Ki

Ku

243

Uath Lochans to Feshiebridge

Walk Data

Orientation
Circuit route

Length
2.8 miles (4.5 km)

Grade
● Easy

Time
1½ hours

Height Gain
90m (328ft)

Hills & Steeps
Long hill

Terrain
Hard and natural

Markings
▶ Blue marker

Wheelchairs
No access

Access for Prams
Not suitable

Key Features

Woodland trail with varied wildlife

Good View points

Ant Hills

Uath Lochans

Noise Indicator

Forest noise mixed with the odd car.

Start the walk from the lochans car park

This is a walk through part of the Inshriach Forest, once owned by the Duke of Gordon's estate but now administered by the Forestry Commission after its purchase in 1935. The woods contain rare Caledonian Scots pine.

The walk from the Uath Lochans is a decent length but by no means a troubling one. You certainly don't need to tog up in expensive walking attire, or carry one of those nerdy ski poles. If you are heavy on your legs just pick up a stick - the woods are full of them – and, note, it's far better for the environment to use natural materials. What's more they're free and biodegradable, unlike metallic poles carrying stickers with designer name!

You can choose to do this as a circuit walk or one way, but remember there is no public transport, so you will need to make arrangements for collecting your car from the start.

From the car park at the lochans, follow back along the access road following the blue markers. When you come to the junction, cross over the road and turn left down the path along the trees and road. Walk for half a mile and eventually you are directed right and into the woods along a vehicle track. Walk uphill and after a short distance you turn left up a smaller path at a blue marker post. Follow the route, keeping to the blue markers: you enter various woods and a clearing before passing the Balcraggan B&B on your left. At this point don't go to the road but turn left and head back uphill, staying on the vehicle track. You continue all the way along until you meet up with the out-going section of the path, after which you follow your steps back to the car park at the start.

This is a quiet walk through a wood heaving with woodland dwellers and alive with birdsong. Look down at your feet along the path and you will see thousands of ants hard at work.

 There are no concerns for dog walkers. Let them run.

Location: Take the access road of the B970 left at Insh House.

Barn Owl

Extras

 Free parking is available at the start of the walk.

 No public toilets, the nearest are at the Loch Insh centre, 1-1/2 miles away. Patrons only

 Nearest:
Accommodation - All Kincraig.
Ossian Hotel (01540) 651 242.
Loch Insh Centre 01540 651 272
visit - www.visitkincraig.com
Food - Ossian Hotel (01540) 651 242.
Loch Insh Centre 01540 651 272
Fuel Station - Aviemore 7 miles.

 Contact for further details:
www.forestry.gov.uk

Ki

Ku

Birch Woodie (The Hazel Woods)

Walk Data

 Orientation
Circuit route

 Length
1.2 miles (2 km)

 Grade
● Easy

 Time
25 minutes

 Height Gain
Minimal

 Hills & Steeps
Steep hill

 Terrain
Natural path

Markings
▶ Blue arrows

Wheelchairs
No access

Access for Prams
Not suitable

Key Features

🌿 Wood water trail
with varied wildlife

🦌 Varied Wildlife

🌊 River Gynack

Noise Indicator

🔊 Gushing water and
lots of bird song.

Start near the doctors surgery area

Birch Woodie or, as it's also known locally, the Hazel Wood, is a small one running by the River Gynack, which gushes down from Loch Gynack and flows in to the Spey at a point close to the high school.

The woods are split by the river, which cuts through rocky gorges as it goes. In parts the rock-faces are very steep, forming various ledges which help to create small waterfalls.

In places the torrent is hidden from view due by the steep sides of the gorge and the thick vegetation growing along the river path.

With easy access to the wood off Gynack Road, this woodland trail is not a hard one and, being so close to the village centre, it's a perfect family type outing which will help while away the spare time.

There are number of points where you can join the walk via a bridge crossing of Gynack Road, all of which are well sign posted. The route is also way-marked with a blue arrow and it's soon noticeable how wild Birch Woodie actually is. The trees and vegetation are thick and run amok to form tunnels with overhanging branches, roots criss-crossing and breaking the path's natural terrain, which when wet gets very muddy in places. The are numerous short paths off the main track, some even leading down to the water's edge, arriving on rocky shelves which can be dangerous, with steep drops into the water. As with the path, if it's raining the rocks could be very slippery, so caution is advised at all times.

Around the woods you may well see or hear a number of wood-dwelling birds. Red squirrels can also be seen scurrying around.

 For obvious reasons, keep man's best friend close to you near the water's edge.

Location: Ardvonie Car Park is located off Gynack Road next to the doctor's surgery, which is behind the Duke of Gordon Hotel.

Wood Warbler

Extras

 Parking is available in the Ardvonie car park next to the surgery.

There are public toilets next to the car park and surgery..

Nearest:
Accommodation - Lots of hotels, B&B's etc around Kingussie.
visit - www.kingussie.co.uk
Food - Around Kingussie
Fuel Station - In Newtonmore 4 miles away.

i Contact for further details:
Ralia Visitor Centre
(01540) 673 907

Ki
Ku

Creag Bheag Trail

Walk Data

Orientation
Circuit route

Length
3.7 miles (6 km)

Grade
● Challenging

Time
2 hours

Height Gain
257m (843ft)

Hills & Steeps
Very steep hill

Terrain
Natural, rocks, tarmac

Markings
▶ Purple arrows

Wheelchairs
No access

Access for Prams
Not suitable

Key Features

Wood & moors with varied wildlife

Good View points

Golf Course

Loch Gynack

Noise Indicator

Bird song and wind rush on a windy day.

Start near the doctors surgery area

Overlooking Kingussie is Creag Bheag, rising to 1600 feet (486m) and giving a 360-degree panoramic views for miles, including a clear view down to Loch Gynack.

The circular walk over Creag Bheag is going to test your mettle for sure, and if you get dizzy at heights or are totally burgered on fatty fast foods then stay away - this is no Toy Town toddle. It's not that this is a long hike, far from it, but there is a section to test the best, and good footwear is an absolute must. It should also be said that novices should not tackle this walk, especially on a wet or windy day.

Doing the walk in an anti-clock wise direction is the best option, as you will get the steep rock climb out of the way early on, leaving a sedate trail back down. Begin from the car park at the doctor's surgery and walk up to the golf course. When you come to the caravan park, turn left at the way-marker post pointing you to the edge of the woods, at which you turn right and follow a very rough and uneven path through woods and heather. At one point you come to an enormous stile, which you pass over and bear right. After an uphill walk you will eventually come to a signpost with the two options, left or right.

Violet Ground Beetle

Go right and you have an easy walk back down around the golf course, but go left and you will soon be going into billy-goat mode with the path suddenly going up a steep hill, which will see you clambering over embedded rocks surrounded by heather. Eventually, after a lot of huffing and puffing, the path tapers off and you will arrive at the top, where there are a number of cairns and great views to saviour. The way back down is far easier - you simply follow the well-worn track back to Kingussie, with the final stage through a pinewood.

Extras

 Parking is available in the Ardvonie car park next to the surgery.

 There are public toilets next to the car park and surgery.

 Nearest:
Accommodation - Lots of hotels, B&B's etc around Kingussie.
visit - www.kingussie.co.uk
Food - Around Kingussie
Fuel Station - In Newtonmore 4 miles away.

 No worries for walking the dog, unless it's unfit...

Location: Ardvonie Car Park is located off Gynack Road next to the doctor's surgery, which is behind the Duke of Gordon Hotel.

Contact for further details:
Ralia Visitor Centre
(01540) 673 907

Ki
Ku

249

Insh Marshes - Invertromie Trail

Kingussie

see walk diagram on map page 228

Walk Data

Orientation
Circuit route

Length
2.3 (4.5kms)

Grade
● Easy

Time
2 hours

Height Gain
Minimal

Hills & Steeps
Short hills

Terrain
Soft natural paths

Markings
▶ White marker

Wheelchairs
No access

Access for Prams
Not suitable

Key Features

Wood & river trail with varied wildlife

Bird Hides

Nature Reserve

River Tromie

Noise Indicator

Lots of bird song with the odd vehicle.

Start from the Insh Marshes car park

The Insh Marshes, which stretch between Kingussie and Kincraig, are one of the most important wetland areas in Europe, proving breeding and feeding grounds for so many different birds - including goldeneyes (half their UK population breed here).

The Invertromie trail is a simple walk that children will love, offering lots of opportunities to see many birds from viewpoints and hides. The walk starts from the car park at the marshes information centre and twists and turns along a trail with no concerns in terms of steep hills or obstacles to surmount. There are no un-bridged rivers or burns to clear and in general the whole walk is well looked after and extremely well signposted. However, this is a walk which goes through an area of land that floods regularly, so parts it the trail can be very muddy and boggy when it rains - decent footwear is called for.

From the car park, head up the wooden steeps and follow the white marker posts around a trail that involves some small hills and numerous gates. At numbered points near the start you can pull off the main track and visit one of the hides or sit at a picnic table viewpoint. Along the river section of the walk you will not only be able to smell the Speyside Distillery - look across the River Tromie and you can see the mashing house. The final stretch of the walk is through a field, which you enter as directed by the post. Keep to the wall and follow the fence and eventually you'll come to the gate which leads to the starting point.

Goldeneye

Insh Marshes attracts lots of wading and water birds such as lapwings, redshanks, whooper swans, mallards, wigeons and spotted crakes. There are hides and a viewing gallery to see the birds. Midges are also common here, so expect to get bitten!

 This is an area of ground-breeding birds and where livestock may be in fields, so keep dogs under control.

Location: The access car park is reached off the B970 a mile outside Kingussie.

Extras

 Free parking is available at the start of the walk.

 No public toilets, the nearest are in Kingussie near the doctors surgery, 1 mile away.

 Nearest:
Accommodation - Lots of hotels, B&B's etc in Kingussie 1 mile away. visit - www.kingussie.co.uk
Food - Various restaurants, cafes and tea rooms in Kingussie, 1 mile away.
Fuel Station - Newtonmore 6 miles.

Contact for further details: www.rspb.org.uk/scotland

Ki
Ku

251

Jubilee Walk to Ruthven Barracks

Kingussie   see walk diagram on map page 227

Walk Data

Orientation
Point to point

Length (one way)
1.2 miles (2 km)

Grade
● Easy

Time (one way)
20 minutes

Height Gain
Minimal

Hills & Steeps
Flat

Terrain
Tarmac & surfaced

Markings
► Pink arrow

Wheelchairs
Good access

Access for Prams
Easy access

Key Features

Road trail with varied wildlife

Good View points

Historic Building

River Spey

Noise Indicator

Lots of road noise from nearby traffic.

Start near the doctors surgery area

The local jaunt known as the 'Jubilee Walk' is as about as easy as it gets, and should you not be able to find the barracks, if you get lost on this trail then you need to see a shrink!!

The walk starts in the centre of Kingussie at the Ardvonie Car Park, off Gynack Road. From here turn right down the road and cross over the high street, turn right again and walk along the top of the village green at the end of which you turn left and walk down to the station.

After passing the Silverfjord Hotel and crossing over the railway line, you walk past the High School along a side track. When you come to the shinty pitch on your right you can peel off and walk around it, otherwise continue straight on over the bridge crossing the Spey. As the road bends the Barracks will come into view -you'll see the entrance path opposite the car park. The current Ruthven Barracks was built in 1719, but this was not the original build - a castle sat here in 1229.

Because of the Jacobite uprisings of 1715, the government and king of the day decided that measures had to be taken to deter or deal with any further riotous behaviour by the Scots, so large numbers of government troops were stationed all over the Highlands. The utterly ruthless Honoverians were fated to leave Badenoch with an utterly roofless hangover, but in its hey-day the building held up to 120 offi-cers and troops, who were kept on stand-by at all times. The strong-hold was regularly fought over and in August 1745 an army of 200-odd Jacobites were held at bay by just 12 government redcoat troops, who won the battle with the loss of just one soldier. The Jacobites did capture the barracks in 1746, but after the defeat at the Battle of Culloden they set fire to the place and fled. What remains now is pretty much what was left in 1746.

 The walk takes you along, and close to, a main road, so keep your dog on the lead.

Location: Follow the signs for Insh and Kincraig along B970.

Red Coat Soldier

Extras

 Parking is available in the Ardvonie car park next to the surgery.

There are public toilets next to the car park and surgery. 20p entry.

Nearest:
Accommodation - Lots of hotels, B&B's etc around Kingussie.
visit - www.kingussie.co.uk
Food - Around Kingussie
Fuel Station - In Newtonmore 4 miles away.

 Contact for further details:
www.historic-scotland.gov.uk

Ki

Ku

253

Kingussie Golf Course Circular

Kingussie

see walk diagram on map page 228

Walk Data

Orientation
Circut route

Length
1½ miles (2.5km)

Grade
● Easy

Time
1½ hours

Height Gain
130m (427ft)

Hills & Steeps
Steep at first

Start near the doctors surgery area

Terrain
Natrual and tarmac

Markings
► Yellow

Wheelchairs
No access

Access for Prams
Not suitable

Key Features

Woodland trail with varied wildlife

Good View points

Golf Course

Loch Gynack

Noise Indicator

Groans from irate golfers.

Kingussie Golf Course dates back to around 1891 and sits high above the village, with a craggy hill proving a stunning backdrop.

Being a popular golf course with locals, they take their game very seriously here - the art of hitting a little white ball on this hillside is not something to be ridiculed and many golfers (check out the trousers - such style!) would prefer that the walkers were kept far away. Perhaps that's why much of the walk is well clear of the course altogether, and runs through bordering forests and woods.

You can do this walk clockwise or anti-clockwise. The better option is clockwise - it's far more interesting, taking you up a fairly tough hill path along a very uneven track with tree roots poking through for much of the initial route, and if it's not roots then there are rocks and bogs to contend with.

Begin from the car park at the doctor's surgery and walk up to the golf course. At the caravan park, turn left at the way-marker post pointing you to the edge of the woods, where you turn right and follow the path following the yellow arrows. The path twists and turns, taking you uphill with some tricky parts here and there, including a boggy area just after the large stile, where there is also a through gate.

Brambling

After an initially tough uphill walk you'll eventually come to a two-way signpost directing you to turn right towards the top of the course, which initially takes you very close to the shoreline of Loch Gynack. Continue following the yellow markers through the woods and you will soon come out onto part of the course near some old buildings, before being taken back around the outside of the course and along the Gynack Burn to finish up walking along a tarmac road to the car park, which will take you across a bridge built by the army.

Extras

 Parking is available in the Ardvonie car park next to the surgery.

 The nearest public toilets are a mile away near the doctors surgery.

 Nearest:
Accommodation - Lots of hotels, B&B's etc around Kingussie.
visit - www.kingussie.co.uk
Food - At the golf club
Fuel Station - In Newtonmore 4 miles away.

Dogs should be kept on the lead around the sections close to the golf course.

Location: To reach the start at the Caravan site, turn up Gynack Street, and drive on for a mile.

Contact for further details:
Ralia Visitor Centre
(01540) 673 907

KI
Ku

Ruthven Barracks & Glen Tromie

Kingussie

see walk diagram on map page 227

Walk Data

Orientation
Circuit route

Length
6 miles (9.6 km)

Grade
● Challenging

Time
2¾ hours

Height Gain
160m (525ft)

Hills & Steeps
Long inclines

Terrain
Natural & tarmac

Markings
None to follow

Wheelchairs
No access

Access for Prams
Not suitable

Key Features

Woodland trail with varied wildlife

Good View points

Historic Building

River Tromie

Noise Indicator

Quiet walk with various bird sounds.

Start opposite Ruthven Barracks

If you are not good at following unkept paths through moorland heather, or don't have good directional awareness, then give this walk a miss and do the history tour of Ruthven Barracks instead, because some navigational skills are required, right from the outset.

Start the walk from the lay-by which looks down on the car park opposite Ruthven Barracks. At the top are two gates leading into fields, take the right-hand gate and walk to the top of the hill. The track disappears early on, so when you get to the top, look for the mobile phone mast to your left and electric pylons ahead. You aim for the pylons at the point where they near a ruin. Once in view you walk towards the disused house keeping a look out the track ahead in the heather. Just past the building you jump across a small burn before picking up the track, while all the time noting that the phone mast is well to your left.

Follow the path through the heather as it heads up hill at times becoming very soft and boggy. Eventually the path runs up to a fence with a thin wood on the other side. You scale the fence via the steps and head down hill. At the bottom of the woods you will see a house which you head for passing through a gate on your right. Through the gate, turn left along the Keepers House and over a wooden bridge, before turning left again passing the 'Danger Snakes' sign. From here you walk along the tarmac road until you come to the bridge over the River Tromie. Turn left over the bridge and a few yards ahead, you will see a gate on your right, pass through and follow the trail to the left which soon comes to a steped and lined hill. Head up the hill and follow the path via a number of gates through a wood and heather patch until it comes out at a gate opposite a field. Pass through the gate and at the main road turn right and walk back to Ruthven Barracks, which is about 20 minutes ahead.

Peacock

Great walk for the dog off the lead, apart form the first field where there may be sheep.

Location: Ruthven Barracks is a mile from Kingussie on the B970.

Extras

Parking is available in the Ardvonie car park next to the surgery.

The nearest public toliets are in Kingussie, 1 mile away at the doctor's surgery. 20p entry.

Nearest:
Accommodation - Lots of hotels, B&B's etc around Kingussie.
visit - www.kingussie.co.uk
Food - Around Kingussie
Fuel Station - In Newtonmore 4 miles away.

Contact for further details:
Ralia Visitor Centre
(01540) 673 907

Ki
Ku

257

Tom Baraidh Walk

Walk Data

Orientation
Circuit route

Length
2.5 miles (4 km)

Grade
● Easy

Time
1½ hours

Height Gain
78m (226ft)

Hills & Steeps
Easy hiil

Terrain
Natural path

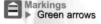

Markings
▶ Green arrows

Wheelchairs
No access

Access for Prams
Not suitable

Key Features

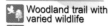

Woodland trail with
varied wildlife

Golf Course

River Gynack

Noise Indicator

Lots of road noise
from nearby A9.

Start near the doctors surgery area

The Tom Baraidh is a fine forest walk incorporating a stretch of road constructed by General Wade in 1714 as part of the government's campaign against the rebellious highlanders.

The walk can be done as a long circuit from the Ardvonie Car Park, next to the doctor's surgery, heading past the golf course at the top of Gynack Road, or simply point-to-point for the north end of the village opposite the A9 slip road.

As a full circuit, the walk will take about an hour and a half at a gentle pace. Begin along Gynack Road, towards the golf course. As you near the car park at the top of the hill, on your right you will see a marker post directing you over a small bridge crossing the river Gynack. After crossing over via the bridge built by the army, turn left and walk up the tarmac road running by the golf course and the river.

Half-way up this stretch you'll come to a large opening on your right with a sign pointing you into the woods. Just inside the trees you'll see a green marker post on your left opposite a large shed. At this point, turn left and follow the track as directed. A short way in you will come to a point where the route splits: if you take the path to your right, you will go deeper into the woods only to remerge at a point near the end of them. Either way, you leave the wood at the sign pointing towards Kingussie. Follow this route to continue the full circuit passing over a stile and trough some gates that lead down to the main road into the village, before returning to the car park.

Parts of the trail can be soft, especially when it's raining, so boots may be needed. The walk is also not good for prams, and towards the end of the trail, birdsong is replaced by the roar of vehicles on the A9.

 Dogs are free to run through the woods, but take care near the golf course and the roads.

Location: Ardvonie Car Park is found just off Gynack Road.

Goldcrest

Ki
Ku

Extras

 Parking is available in the Ardvonie car park next to the surgery.

 The nearest public toliets are a mile away near the surgery. 20p entry.

Nearest:
Accommodation - Lots of hotels, B&B's etc around Kingussie.
visit - www.kingussie.co.uk
Food - At the golf club
Fuel Station - In Newtonmore 4 miles away.

Contact for further details:
Ralia Visitor Centre
(01540) 673 907

259

West Terrace Circular

Kingussie

Walk Data

Orientation
Circuit route

Length
1.6 miles (2.5 km)

Grade
● Easy

Time
1 hour

Height Gain
120m (394ft)

Hills & Steeps
Steep hill section

Terrain
Natural & tarmac

Markings
▶ Red arrow

Wheelchairs
No access

Access for Prams
Not suitable

Key Features

Woodland trail with varied wildlife

Start near the doctor's surgery area

This walk comes in three parts - part one through a wood, part two along the woods and part three nowhere near the woods.

The walk takes you into a pine forest that's not so dense that daylight is blocked out. The walk is easily reached from the Ardvonie Car Park and overall involves going up the hill and, just like Jack, back down again (but you'll not be needing the vinegar and brown paper).

Part one, and starting the walk from the car park in an anti clockwise direction, you walk up the short track to the right of the public toilets. At the top of the hill turn right as directed by the wooden signpost. A short way along, you enter the woods to your left via a gate.

As soon as you get into woods the path heads uphill all the way, until you leave the trees. The track is very rough in places, which in fact all

Noise Indicator

Lots of bird sounds plus faint road noise.

260

goes to enhance the walk's appeal. After winding your way up a wide track lined by the trees, you encounter near the top part of the path a surface lined with over-stones and shingle, all washed down by heavy rainfalls.

Eventually you come to a gate on the edge of the woods. Pass through and turn left, to begin the third part of the journey, which from here is all downhill, along a bumpy track with rocks jutting up from the ground. With the path on the outside of the woods next to a stone wall at the bottom of the hill, you come to a gate next to a building. At this point you turn left onto the tarmac and begin the third and final part of the circuit, which is a simple stroll via some houses, on a flat road, and a downhill path.

Ki

Ku

Extras

 Parking is available in the Ardvonie car park next to the surgery.

Like any woods, this one is alive with all sorts of inhabitants, birds pleasingly audible. As you go along, lift any stone or piece of dead or rotting wood and you'll see all kinds of creatures.

 There are public toilets next to the car park and surgery.

 Nearest:
Accommodation - Lots of hotels, B&B's etc around Kingussie.
visit - www.kingussie.co.uk
Food - Around Kingussie
Fuel Station - In Newtonmore 4 miles away.

 No worries for Fido, but do respect the homes en route.

 Contact for further details:
Ralia Visitor Centre
(01540) 673 907

Location: Ardvonie Car Park is located off Gynack Road next to the doctor's surgery.

261

Laggan & Newtonmore

Laggan and Newtonmore are situated on the southern western border of the Cairngorms National Park, with Laggan along the A86 - the last village in the western side of the park - and Newtonmore located just off the A9 next to the River Spey.

Over the last few years this place became very well known thanks to the hit BBC serial "Monarch of the Glen", which was filmed on location all around the area using some of stunning locations as open film sets. The programme was set on the shores of Loch Laggan and it's easy to understand why anyone would want to set a novel here.

The walks to be had here are fantastic and offer something for everyone. If you want a simple village stroll, take the Wildcat Trail around Newtonmore, which can be done as one whole walk or split into sections.

A particularly good walk is the Blackwood & Pictish Fort in Laggan, but it's a tester for sure. On the other hand, the Gorstean Crag Walk in Laggan is a fine, easy family one through a thick and open forest.

One of the easiest in the area is the Loch Imrich trail in Newtonmore, simply perfect for a 20 minute stroll.

Allt Mhoraich Trail (see page 266)

Glen Truim Woods & View Point Walk (see page 272)

Blackwood & the Pictish Fort Walk (see page 268)

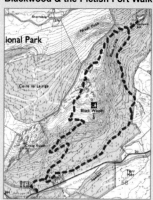

Gorstean Crag Walk (see page 274)

Laggan Spey River Walk (see page 276)

Druim An Aird & Pattack Falls (see page 279)

Cat of 6 Trails (see page 278) and the Wild Cat Circular (see page 284)

Highland Folk Museum History Tour(see page 280)

L
N

Loch Imrich
(see page 282)

Allt Mhoraich Trail

Laggan see walk diagram on map page 264

Walk Data

Orientation
Circuit route

Length
3.4 miles (5.5km)

Grade
● Moderate

Time
1¾ hours

Height Gain
200m (656ft)

Hills & Steeps
Long hill

Terrain
Natural paths

Markings
▶ Orange arrows

Wheelchairs
No access

Access for Prams
Not suitable

Key Features

Moorland hill trail
with varied wildlife

Good View points

Burn

Noise Indicator

Quiet walk with only
natural sounds.

Start the walk from Woods of Breakachy.

The walk snakes it way around a high crag and across open heather moorland, with a few trees at the start. This is quite a barren walk, that takes you up hill and down again, but to be honest, you only lose sight of civilisation for a short while as you negotiate the rear of the path, as it traverses the hilly crag - the rest of the time you can see much of Laggan in the distance along the valley.

Rated as a moderate walk, if you have a keen sense of direction then you may well actually find this an easy one. The main reason for the moderate grading has more to do with navigation due to the fact that some of the marker arrow posts have either disappeared or are not in place, you have to make your own judgements on the actual direction. But that said, because this walk is lined in part by a high deer fence, it's almost impossible to get lost as the fence naturally directs you back down to the road. Just bear in mind that you are walking clockwise around a high hill with a crag, and it should always be in your centre as you go and to your right.

Begin the walk for the gate on the road, and pass through heading straight up hill through a few trees and over soft ground. Initially there are marker posts spread out along a faint track that often disappears as you walk through the heather moorland which forms 90% of the trail. As you approach the deer fence, which you bear right and follow along behind the hill, the posts seem to disappear, however once you round the hill you can simply follow the fence until the road ahead comes into view, at which point you simply walk to it, turning right at the road once you get to it in order to return to the start. You can also use the home wind generator as a marker and head for it, noting to bear right on to the road when you are able to.

You may well spot roe deer in the heather or buzzards above.

The landowner requests no dogs due to young livestock.

Location: 3 miles off the A9 along the Glen Trumin and Laggan road.

Roe Deer

Extras

There is no official parking at the start of the walk, with only a small layby and road passing spaces, which farmers and locals won't thank you for blocking off. However, along the road you will find spots to park.

The nearest toilets are in Laggan 4 miles away.

Nearest:
Accommodation - Numerous B&B's, 2 hotels and self-catering available around the village.
visit - www.laggan.com
Food - Laggan 4 miles.
Fuel Station - Newtonmore 8 miles

L

Blackwood & the Pictish Fort Walk

Walk Data

Orientation
Circuit route

Length
5 miles (8 km)

Grade
● Challenging

Time
2½ hours

Height Gain
315m (1033ft)

Hills & Steeps
Long steeps

Terrain
Natural paths

Markings
▶ Blue arrows

Wheelchairs
No access

Access for Prams
Not suitable

Key Features

Wood & hill trail with varied wildlife

Good View points

Historic Fort

Noise Indicator

90% quiet walk, with the odd car sound.

Start the walk from Druim an Aird Car Park.

The is a memorable walk for many reasons, notably the steep one-hour uphill initial section and the stunning panoramic views from the summit. And what about the ancient Pictish Fort perched high up on a steep rock face...?

If you haven't got a head for heights or break out in a sweat after walking the length of your own body, then visit the wee pond next to the Laggan shop, for this walk isn't for you! As well as gaining in height to a level of 565m at the summit, the walk up is long, arduous, uphill slog for at least an hour before it levels out, and when you get to the top you will be ready for a rest. That said, you don't actually need to be a billy goat or a badly-dressed townie on a weekend walking trip to conquer the full circuit - but it is important to point out that this is a stout walk on tough terrain, so good footwear is essential, especially for the section down to the fort, or if it has been raining.

Starting from Pattack Falls, from the car park cross over the road and behind a small clump you will come across a fence with an opening: note the marker post is missing here; however, pass through and walk into a very dark section and after just a short distance you will see a signpost. From this point follow the Hill Top and Fort trail which takes you up to the summit via a TV mast, before dropping down to the Dun Da Lamh Fort, which is marked with an information plaque detailing the fort's origins. There is a short spur trail up to the fort, which takes 5 minutes to reach. After viewing the ruins you walk back to the main trail and then continue back down following the sign for Achduchil and Pattack along a wide vehicle track through a very dark pinewood and an open plane.

The woods are alive with lots of creatures from furry to scary. Red squirrels and foxes live alongside the deer, hares and rabbits; black grouse are also around, as are redstarts and buzzards.

 Excellent walk all the way with the dog off the lead.

Location: The Druim an Aird car park is 5 miles south of Laggan.

Garden Tiger Moth Caterpillar

Extras

 Free parking at Druim an Aird Car park which is across the road opposite the start, 4 miles from Laggan Stores.

 The nearest public toilets are in Laggan 5 miles away.

 Nearest:
Accommodation - Numerous B&B's, 2 hotels and self-catering available around the village.
visit - www.laggan.com
Food - Laggan 4 miles.
Fuel Station - Newtonmore 8 miles

Druim An Aird & Pattack Falls

Walk Data

Orientation
Circuit route

Length
1.2 miles (2.3km)

Grade
● Easy

Time
1 hour

Height Gain
100m (328ft)

Hills & Steeps
One main steep

Terrain
Natural path

Markings
▶ Red arrow

Wheelchairs
No access

Access for Prams
Not suitable

Key Features

Woodland hill trail
with varied wildlife

Good View points

Pattack Falls

Noise Indicator

Water-fall rush and
lots of bird song.

🌀 **Start the walk from Druim an Aird Car Park.**

The Druim An Aird trail is a walk with history and a fast waterfall, which collectively will make for a fine afternoon's stretch and learn.

Located approximately 5 miles south of the Laggan stores is Strathmashie Forest, a community-led project where you can walk along well-tended paths, or simply stand and savour the sights of the Pattack Falls, a narrow gorge that was used as a film location in the BBC's hit television series, 'Monarch of the Glen'.

Before heading off and doing the main trail, if you hike up the short path leading off the car park you will soon come to the falls which you can observe from a viewing platform surrounded by a safety fence which allows you to peer down directly over the water with clear views, as the water cascades down over jagged rocks en-route to Loch Laggan.

Once you have seen the falls, follow the red arrow markers up the trail, which soon comes to a small wooden bridge. Shortly after you will come to a junction: turn left and follow the loop walk that will take you past the ancient ruins of the Druim An Aird village, via a hill walk and through a thick pine wood. After walking up a steep section, the trail mellows out in to a clearing revealing the ruins ahead.

Soay Sheep

Druim An Aird, which is said to translate, as 'High Ridge' is an abandoned settlement dating back to around the 1700s. Today all that is left is a collection of stone shells laid out as they were left. There is an information plaque giving the village history placed next to a viewpoint and seating area. From the site, simply follow the marker posts back to the start, which will take you back in to the woods.

Extras

 Free parking at Druim an Aird Car park which is across the road opposite the start, 4 miles from Laggan Stores.

 The nearest toilets are in Laggan 5 miles away.

As well as lots of traditional wildlife found here, you can also see soay sheep, a small brown breed originating from the western Isles of Scotland.

 Nearest:
Accommodation - Numerous B&B's, 2 hotels and self-catering available around the village.
visit - www.laggan.com
Food - Laggan 4 miles.
Fuel Station - Newtonmore 8 miles

 Good walk all the way round with Fido free of his lead.

Location: The Druim an Aird car park is 5 miles south of Laggan.

271

Glen Truim Woods & View Point Trail

Laggan   see walk diagram on map page 264

Walk Data

Orientation
Circuit route

Length
1.9 (3 km)

Grade
● Easy

Time
1 hour

Height Gain
120m (394ft)

Hills & Steeps
Steep sections

Terrain
Natural

Markings
▶ Blue arrow

Wheelchairs
No access

Access for Prams
Not suitable

Key Features

Woodland hill trail with varied wildlife

Good View points

🕐 Start the walk at Creagan an Fhithich.

The most notable thing here is the noise which comes from vehicles hurtling along the busy Perth-Inverness trunk road less than a quarter of a mile away. However, don't let the road noise put you off, because for those who get off on hill views, this walk is going to satisfy your fetish big style. The walk is not hard and is set out along wide vehicle tracks for at least 75% of the way, winding through fairly open pine forest. Much of the trail is uphill and there is one steep section up to the viewpoint to contend with.

Start the walk from the access road off the A9 reached by travelling south from Newtonmore to the turn off for Laggan and Glen Truim. Immediately after the junction travel over the bridge spanning the River Truim, and head uphill passing the Invernahavon Caravan Site. A quarter of a mile on, on your right you will see a lay-by in to the woods with a stile.

Noise Indicator

Lots of noise from the A9 road traffic.

Cross the stile and follow the blue marker arrows along the very wide loggers' vehicle track uphill, looking out for red squirrels and great spotted woodpeckers as you go. After 30 minutes, and as the road noise fades, you will come to a junction with a sign pointing you up to the View Point trail, one way up a hill section that takes about 20 minutes to reach the top from the junction. This part of the walk is steep and a few sweat beads may well appear by the time you get to the top, where you will find a bench and a stone cairn.

Great Spotted Woodpecker

Once you have had your fill, simply retrace your steps back down to the junction, at which point you can ether take the main track to the left down to the road, where you turn right and walk back to the start, or follow on up the small trail that continues through the woods. Note the smaller track is not officially part of the trail and it can be a bit rough.

 For dog walkers there are no concerns apart form the short stretch along the road to the end, where there will be livestock and cars to look out for.

Location: Two miles south of Newtonmore off the A9 to the Glen Trumin and Laggan road.

Extras

 Very limited un-official parking is available next to the start of the walk at the gates.

 Nearest loos are in Newtonmore 2 miles away.

Nearest:
Accommodation - Numerous B&B's, hotels and self-catering available in Laggan or Newtonmore
visit - www.laggan.com
visit - www.newtonmore.com
Food - Laggan and Newtonmore.
Fuel Station - Newtonmore 2 miles north turning off the A9.

L

Gorsten Crag Walk

Walk Data

Orientation
Circuit route

Length
1 mile (1.8Km)

Grade
● Easy

Time
1¼ hours

Height Gain
168m (551ft)

Hills & Steeps
Steep sections

Terrain
Natural path

Markings
▶ White arrow

Wheelchairs
No access

Access for Prams
Not suitable

Key Features

Woodland hill trail with varied wildlife

Good View points

Picnic Table

Noise Indicator

Quiet walk with only bird song en-route

Start the walk from Druim an Aird Car Park.

The Gorsten walk is a really nice forest ramble which, despite being rated as easy, is nevertheless a bit sweat-breaking, with a notably steep hill to conquer whether you navigate the circuit clockwise or anticlockwise.

This short circular trail starts from the Gorsten Car Park, 2 miles south of Laggan and travels along a good path which starts out on a wide, hard base, but once you head off the main track the ground is much softer. You'll head uphill into the trees on a natural earth-based, uneven and often narrow track. But don't fret, this is an excellent trail and despite its not being suitable at all for someone pushing a pram or in a wheelchair, only those who are really unfit will find the walk too hard. The steps only last for a short section, but you'll be pufing and sweating as you go before reaching the top at the picnic table.

Begin the walk from the car park through a thick wood. Initially the path is quite sedate regarding gradient, but after a few hundred metres you will come to a marker post with an arrow directing you to go left. It's from this point that things suddenly get tough, because the track narrows and steepens sharply. Follow the white arrow into the woods and eventually after a steep rise you will come to the point where things mellow, leading to a picnic table at a good viewpoint. After chilling and getting your breath, set off again following the arrows which will take you back down through the woods, passing thick, tall pines on either side. Eventually the path opens out into a clearing and having crossed the small bridge you will come to the main track with a sign opposite the Wolf Trax cycleway: turn right and follow the path back down to the start.

In the woods and around the walk you may be lucky enough to see or hear black grouse as well as various deer including sika.

 Excellent leadless walk for dogs, with no concerns.

Location: The Gorsten car park is 2 miles south of Laggan Stores.

Sika Deer

Extras

 Free parking at Druim an Aird Car park which is across the road opposite the walks start, 4 miles from Laggan Stores.

 The nearest toilets are in Laggan 4 miles away.

 Nearest:
Accommodation - Numerous B&B's, 2 hotels and self-catering available around the village.
visit - www.laggan.com
Food - Laggan 4 miles.
Fuel Station - Newtonmore 8 miles

L

Laggan River Spey Walk

Walk Data

Orientation
Circuit route

Length
1.7 miles (2.8km)

Grade
● Easy

Time
1 hour

Height Gain
Minimal

Hills & Steeps
Small gradient

Terrain
Soft natural path

Markings
▶ Pink arrows

Wheelchairs
No access

Access for Prams
Not suitable

Key Features

Riverside trail with varied wildlife

Good View points

River Spey

Noise Indicator

Quiet walk with some road noise.

Start along Glen Truim to Laggan Road.

The River Spey runs from its barren, remote source, Loch Spey - at 350m above sea level in the Monadhliath Mountains, west of Laggan - and falls over 1100 feet, at a rate of 11.5 feet per mile. Its journey's end, some 105 miles north, is the Moray Firth at Spey Bay.

Not only is this one of the finest rivers in the UK, it's also world-renowned for its fishing, with great catches for salmon and trout annually.

The Spey twists and winds down a path amid ever-changing features, its banks varying considerably - low, easy access sandy banks to steep-sided walls, and stretches where vegetation grows over the shore-line. However, the banks around Laggan and along this walk pose no real problems, and as well as being easy to get to, the views up the valley floor are superb: you can see for miles.

To access the river walk you need to travel along the Glen Truim to Laggan road. Along the road there are a few spots to park a car, but there's no parking at the head of the walk. Once you locate the access gate, some two miles off the A9 exit, you walk down the soft vehicle track, passing a tall pylon. Veering slightly to the right, the path travels down a slight gradient, and since it's not an access point for farm vehicles and live stock, the path can often disappear. But you can get lost; you simply head for the river, which are only a few hundred meters ahead. At the rivers edge turn left and walk along the well-worn riverside path. There is nothing adventurous about this section of the walk and no obstacles. The river meanders along and after a short distance you will come to a gate and fence before heading back up to the road where you turn left and walk along the road to the start point.

The river attracts lots of birds from grey lag geese to oystercatchers.

 The landowner requests on dogs due to young livestock.

Location: 3 miles off the A9 along the Glen Truim and Laggan road.

Extras

 There is no official parking at the start of the walk, with only a small layby and road passing spaces, which farmers and locals won't thank you for blocking off. However, along the road you will find spots to park.

 The nearest loos are in Laggan 4 miles away.

 Nearest:
Accommodation - Numerous B&B's, 2 hotels and self-catering available around the village.
visit - www.laggan.com
Food - Laggan 4 miles.
Fuel Station - Newtonmore 8 miles

277

Cat of 6 Trails

Newtonmore

see walk diagram on map page 265

Walk Data

Orientation
Circuit routes

Length
¾ to 3 miles

Grade
● Easy

Time
1 to 1¼ hours

Height Gain
70m (230ft)

Hills & Steeps
Hilly in places

Terrain
Various

Markings
Black cat signs

Wheelchairs
No access

Access for Prams
Not suitable

Key Features

Woods, moor, river with varied wildlife

Good View points

Rivers Calder & Spey

Noise Indicator

Quiet but broken with road noise.

Start from points around Newtonmore.

The Wildcat Trail can either be completed as one long circuit walk, or split in to a series of shorter connecting trails, all via the village. Splitting the walk into two halves, you could do the trail as a top and bottom walk by following the main Wildcat signs as you go:

1)) Top half, from Banchor Cemetery to Highland Folk Museum and back via the high street. This route will take around 1 hour 15 minutes. (3 miles)

2) The bottom half, from the cemetery via the River Spey, the folk museum and back along the high street. Head across the road from the cemetery and follow the black cat markers which will take you under two bridges, past where two rivers join and along the golf course before re-emerging along the high street and returning to the start. Walk time is 1 hour 15 minutes. (3 miles)

3) The Allt Laraidh is a 40 minute walk from the village centre along Strone road which joins the wild cat trail, taking you past the Allt Laraidh waterfall before bringing you out onto the road. (3⁄4 mile)

4) Calder, Milton & Glen Banchor: a 1-hour walk from Calder Bridge via the cemetery. Following the black cats and then the Calder sign, this walk takes you above the Calder gorge via a short steep hill. (11⁄4 mile)

5) Craggan: a 45-minute walk from the main street. Walk up Glen Road until you come to a cattle grid, follow the signs as directed to a viewpoint where you can see across the Cairngorms. (1 mile)

6) Strone: a 45 minute walk from the village centre via the Balavil Hotel, which takes you up to an area with great views of the Monadhliaths. (1 mile)

Information about the above walks is available from the Wildcat Centre in the high street. Opening times vary, so call to confirm.

Because of livestock in the fields, keep dogs on a lead.

Location: Start off the main street.

Dung Beetle

Extras

 Free parking is available around Newtonmore close to start points.

 Public toliets are located along the high street, 5 minutes from the walk start points.

 Nearest:
Accommodation - Numerous B&B's, hotels, guests houses, hostels etc around the village.
visit - www.newtonmore.com.
Food - All around the villagge
Fuel Station - In the village.

 Contact for further details:
The Wildcat Centre
tel: (01540) 673 131

N

Highland Folk Museum History Tour

Walk Data

Orientation
Circuit route

Length
1 mile

Grade
● Easy

Time
Not specific

Height Gain
Minimal

Hills & Steeps
Flat

Terrain
Surfaced path

Markings
Information boards

Wheelchairs
Good access

Access for Prams
Excellent access

Key Features

Good View points

Picnic Tables

Information Boards

Folk Museum

Noise Indicator

Quiet but broken with road noise.

Start the walk from the car park.

The Highland Folk Museum is an award winning attraction managed by the Highland Council, but owned by the public.

It details the life of highlanders over the centuries from the 1700 to the present day. Using interpretation and activity programmes, the centre brings to life the domestic and working conditions of earlier Highlanders.

Highlanders were a hardy race of people who had to manage in a remote region that was immensely harsh, especially during the winters. You will find out how Highlanders built their homes, farmed their lands and took their the animals to market. You will learn how people in these parts dressed and how hard it was to make ends meet bringing up children with no money, having to trade for food and cloth by bartering livestock etc.

The open-plan history site is located at the north end of the village, with easy access from the main road. There is no set route that you have to follow and if you take your time you could still be learning 4 hours later. Around the site there are number of attractions to visit on foot, setting out from the reception. Features include a 1700's township and a 1930's school, which children can take their place in. There's a farm, a railway hut, a tailor's shop and many more attractions, all with posted details.

The place offers a delightful stroll through a pinewood where red squirrels hang out and often pose for a picture or two. Also among the centre's residents are a couple of friendly, well-fed ponies.

There is good access for wheelchair users, with lift facilities in places. Pram-pushers have no obstacles to worry about, and there's also a kids' play park. There's a fee to enter the site.

 Only guide dogs are allowed around the site, but there's a dog pound with a shelter and drinking water, free of charge.

Location: Enter from the north end of Newtonmore.

Jubilee

Extras

 There is plenty of free parking available at the reception.

 Toilets, with disabled facilities available on site.

 Nearest:
Accommodation - Numerous B&B's, hotels, guests houses, hostels etc around the village. *visit* - www.newtonmore.com
Food - Cafe and shop on site.
Fuel Station - At the south end of the village, 2 minutes drive.

i Contact for further details:
The Highland Folk Museum
tel: (01540) 673 551
www.highlandfolk.com

N

Loch Imrich

Walk Data

 Orientation
Circuit route

 Length
500 metres

 Grade
● Easy

 Time
20 minutes

 Height Gain
Minimal

 Hills & Steeps
One small hill

 Terrain
Natural path

 Markings
None

 Wheelchairs
No access

 Access for Prams
Bumpy

Key Features

 Woods & lochan
with varied wildlife

 Loch Imrich

Noise Indicator

 Quiet but broken
with road noise.

 Start the walk from the bowling green.

Many villages have hidden secrets and Newtonmore is certainly one of them. This wee gem is close to the village centre: Loch Imrich is tucked away in a hollow behind a blanket of trees, and it's an ideal place for a simple stroll, especially with young children.

In the past the loch played host to fishing competitions and during the cold winter months curling was held when its waters had safely frozen - the old wooden curling club hut is still standing close to the water's edge, although it's now boarded up.

Today the loch is used only for relaxation by locals and visitors alike, with the aid of a good path and number of park benches to sit back on and while away the day. The location is very peaceful, with the sounds of singing birds broken by the occasional passing car.

The loch is located just off the high street close to the village centre at north end of Newtonmore. The easiest way to reach the walk is by heading down Golf Course Road directly opposite the Balavil Hotel, next to the Waltzing Waters attraction.

Right opposite the Newtonmore bowling green, 200 yards along, there's a small wooden gate. Pass through it and head down the steps: at the bottom is the main path, which branches out left and right. It makes no matter which way round you walk as the trail meets up at the same point. The path is a natural one with overhanging branches, and on the whole the surface is flat and even. Parents pushing a pram will have an easy time, but you will have to lift the pram down the steps.

The loch attracts various birds with ducks and their offspring regularly bobbing about in the water. Small fish and frogs also breed here and around the site are all sorts of water plants to look out for.

 No obvious restrictions for dog walkers.

Location: Enter from various points off the main street.

Duckling

GOLF COURSE ROAD

N

Extras

 Free parking is available around Newtonmore close to start points.

 Public toliets are located along the high street, 2 minutes from the walk start points.

 Nearest:
Accommodation - Numerous B&B's, hotels, guests houses, hostels etc around the village.
visit - www.newtonmore.com
Food - All around the village
Fuel Station - In the village.

 Contact for further details:
The Wildcat Centre
tel: (01540) 673 131

Wildcat Circular Trail

Walk Data

Orientation
Circuit route

Length
6.2 miles (10 km)

Grade
● Easy

Time
2½ hours

Height Gain
70m (230ft)

Hills & Steeps
Hilly in places

Terrain
Natural and tarmac

Markings
Black wildcat

Wheelchairs
No access

Access for Prams
Not suitable

Key Features

Woods, moor, river
with varied wildlife

Good View points

Rivers Calder & Spey

Noise Indicator

Quiet but broken
with road noise.

🔍 **Start the walk from the Banchor Cemetery.**

First things first: this walk has nothing to do with seeing wild cats! The name derives from the fact that a number of clans associated with Newtonmore use a wildcat in their family crest. There's some evidence of wildcats in the region, but in all honesty you're very unlikely to see any.

The walk - an orbital trail - is maintained by a local trust, which has an information centre in the village where you can get details for all Newtonmore's walks.

The trail is an easy, albeit long one through various elements, from waterside paths with waterfalls to farmland bogs and woods. You will also travel over different types of terrain, where one minute you are walking on hard paths with embedded stones, the next on natural paths that when wet can be very boggy. You will also find yourself walking on tarmac.

A good start point is Banchor Cemetery, off the A86 Laggan road. From the small car park, pick up the trail on the left and simply follow the black-cat marker posts. The path twists and turns and in general it's fairly flat with only one steep hill. You pass through lots of gates en-route, taking you into fields with livestock. After passing a waterfall, the trail brings you out at the main road, and to complete the circuit turn right along the path until you see a white house over the road. Cross over and walk down the road picking up and following the black cat markers again, which will now take you along the River Spey and around part of the golf course. Follow the path past the golf course on your right: you will eventually walk under a rail and road bridge, to end up opposite the start at the cemetery.

Do this walk using the local map and guidance, because there are various short walks attached to the trail with criss-crossing way-signs.

 Because of livestock in fields keep dogs on a lead.

Location: The start of the trail at the cemetery, is two minutes from the village of the A86 to Laggan.

Lapwing

Extras

 Limited free parking is possible near the cemetery.

 Public toilets are located along the high street, 5 minutes from the start point at the cementery.

 Nearest:
Accommodation - Numerous B&B's, hotels, guests houses, hostels etc around the village.
visit - www.newtonmore.com.
Food - All around the villagge
Fuel Station - In the village.

 Contact for further details:
The Wildcat Centre
tel: (01540) 673 131

N

Walked it

Walked It	286 *to* 320
Cairngorm Walking Services	308 *to* 310
Dog Owners	312 *to* 314
Index	316 *to* 318
Scottish Outdoor Access Code	317

"where to now Hamish?'

"you choose Tavish, that last 20 miler has taken its toll on me!"

"I know what you mean, bye the way where's Morag?"

"stuck on a stile 6 miles back"

"she will miss the coach...."

"never mind"

Walked it

Walkers Notes

Stick your own
picture here

Stick your own
picture here

Stick your own
picture here

Stick your own
picture here

Walked it

Walkers Notes

Balliefurth Farm Bed & Breakfast

Location - Grantown-On-Spey

A warm welcome awaits you at Balliefurth, a family run farm on the banks of the famous River Spey. The farmhouse self-catering and B&B with open fires offers the option of an evening meal made with local ingredients including our own beef and lamb. Flexible mealtimes.

Open for: Self catering all year, B&B May-October.

Contact Alastair & Ann MacLennan
tel (01479) 821636
www.scottishholidayhomes.co.uk

Cambus O May Hotel

Location - Ballater

Four miles east of the picturesque village of Ballater, the Cambus O'May Hotel is a haven of peace and tranquillity. All rooms have en-suite facilities. We also have an elegant residents lounge with an open fire and a pine-clad lounge bar. Our dining room is the ideal place to enjoy the excellent cuisine offered from the table d'hote menu which changes daily.

Operating - Open all year

Contact - tel (013397) 55428
www.cambusomayhotel.co.uk

Stick your own
picture here

Stick your own
picture here

Stick your own
picture here

Stick your own
picture here

Walked it

Stick your own
picture here

Stick your own
picture here

Stick your own
picture here

Stick your own
picture here

Lochanhully Woodland Club

MACDONALD
HOTELS & RESORTS

In the great outdoors, enjoy some of the finest pursuits in the Cairngorms located close to our club.

Out There

Walking-
Cycling-
Bird watching-
Orienteering-
Fishing-
Snowsports

Entertainment
Accommodation
Leisure

Restaurant & Bar

Our restaurant is open
from 5pm - 9pm
Lochanhully Woodland
Club House. Carr-bridge
Tel 01479 841 234

Walked it

Walkers Notes

Stick your own
picture here

Stick your own
picture here

Stick your own
picture here

Stick your own
picture here

Glenprosen Holidays

Location - **Glenprosen**
Traditional cosy riverside and moorland
stone cottages in magic locations on the
southernmost edge of Cairngorms
National Park. A large private estate
bursting with wildlife. Blackgame, red
squirrels and otters. Rates from £220 to
£550 per week.
Operating - All year

Contact
tel (01575) 540 302
www.glenprosen.co.uk

Prosen Hostel

Location - **Glenprosen**
Opened 2007 on the southernmost edge of
the Cairngorms National Park.
Comfortable Green Hostel sleeping 18
with family room. Wood burning stove,
internet connection, Drying room and
laundering facilities. Red squirrels outside. £14-18 per person, per night.
Operating - All year

Contact
tel (01575) 540 456
www.prosenhostel.co.uk

Walked it

Walkers Notes

Stick your own
picture here

Stick your own
picture here

Stick your own
picture here

Stick your own
picture here

Walked it

Walkers Notes

Stick your own
picture here

Stick your own
picture here

Stick your own
picture here

Stick your own
picture here

Forestry Commission
Scotland

Walked it

Walkers Notes

Stick your own
picture here

Stick your own
picture here

Stick your own
picture here

Stick your own
picture here

Pinebank Chalets

Pinebank Chalets in Aviemore
offers quality self catering
chalets, apartments, and log
cabin accommodation in the
heart of the Cairngorms National
Park, making this the perfect
location for enjoying outdoor
activities including wildlife tours,
fishing, walking, mountain biking.

Open all year round, we have 5
Log cabins, 8 Chalets & 2
Apartments which can sleep 2-6
people for weekly, weekend and
short break stays.

Contact
tel (01479) 810000
www.pinebankchalets.co.uk

Walked it

Stick your own
picture here

Stick your own
picture here

Stick your own
picture here

Stick your own
picture here

Alvie Estate

Traditional Highland Estate overlooking the Cairngorm mountains
located 4 miles south of Aviemore.

Alvie provides an ideal centre from
which to explore and participate in
one of the many activities available
on or around the Estate.

* Hill Walking
* Skiing
* Golf
* Falconry
* Horse Riding
* Fishing
* Clay Pigeon Shooting
* Archery
* Quad Bike Treks
* Deer Stalking
* Grouse and Hare Shooting
* Gliding
* Watersports

Alvie Estate
Kincraig, Kingussie
(01540) 651 255
Dalraddy Holiday Park
(Chalets, Caravans & Tents)
(01479) 810 330
www.alvie-estate.co.uk

Walked it

Walkers Notes

Stick your own
picture here

Stick your own
picture here

Stick your own
picture here

Stick your own
picture here

Speyside
Leisure Park
Aviemore

**Self catering chalets & caravans
at Aviemore, the heart of the
Highlands of Scotland and the
Cairngorms National Park**

Speyside Leisure Park
Dalfaber Road
Aviemore
Telephone: +44 (0) 1479 810236
Fax: +44 (0) 1479 811688
E-mail:
bookings@speysideleisure.com
www.speysideleisure.com

Walked it

Abernethy Bunkhouse

Stick your own
picture here

Location - Nethy Bridge
Sharing the Speyside Way car park our
centrally heated bunkhouse is well
equipped and has 2 bunkrooms to sleep
up to 9, 1 sleeps 2, plus an extra
bunkroom and store with outside access.
Local activities range from hill-walking and
environmental studies to sightseeing.
Operating - All year round.

Contact
tel (01479) 821 370
www.nethy.org
email: info@nethy.org

Stick your own
picture here

Beechgrove Cottage

Stick your own
picture here

Location - Glenlivet
Three traditional cottages, in different
locations. Set amidst beautiful surround-
ings on the Glen Livet Estate near the
rivers Avon and Livet (fishing available).
Central for the coast, Cairngorms,
Inverness and castle and whisky trails.
There are many local walks and lots of
wildlife to see within easy reach.
Operating - Open all year

Contact
tel (01807) 590 220
email: jaqui154@fsmail.net

Stick your own
picture here

Cairngorm Walking Services

Angus Glens Walking Festival

The Angus Glens Walking Festival is a four-day event offering a varied programme of walks and evening entertainment to suit all ages and abilities.

www.angusanddundee.co.uk/walkingfestival

Aviemore Walking Festival

A full evening programme of events will include mountain related talks, films, Cairngorm Mountain Rescue Team open night, a Ceilidh Supper and the chance to enjoy some of the best of that famous Highland Hospitality! These are also listed under Other Activities. Just follow the link from the Other Info page and also at the bottom of each page.

www.aviemorewalking.com

The Cairngorms National Park Authority

The Cairngorms was made a National Park in September 2003 because it is a unique and special place that needs to be cared for - both for the wildlife and countryside it contains and for the people who live in it, manage it and visit it. It is Britain's largest national Park.

www.cairngorms.co.uk/

Walking at Rothiemurchus

Enjoy some of the most beautiful scenery in Scotland on foot. Rothiemurchus has a 50km network of carefully maintained paths which take you through beautiful forest, around stunning lochs and to the foot of vast mountains.

www.rothiemurchus.net

Walking at Alvie

Alvie & Dalraddy are traditional Highland Estates 4 miles south of Aviemore near the village of Kincraig in Badenoch. The Estate provides an ideal centre from which to explore Scotland and participate in one of the many activities available on the Estate

www.alvie-estate.co.uk

Walking at Balmoral

Set amongst the magnificent scenery of Royal Deeside, in the shadows of Lochnagar is the Balmoral Estate which extends to just over 50,000 acres of heather clad hills and ancient Caledonian woodland. Apart from enjoying the peace and quiet whilst walking through the grounds and gardens around the Castle, visitors can enjoy the marked walks through the woods, up Craig Gowan hill overlooking the Castle and along the riverside.

www.balmoralcastle.com

Stick your own
picture here

Stick your own
picture here

Stick your own
picture here

Stick your own
picture here

GO WILD
IN THE HIGHLANDS

Discover Scotland's wildlife and
endangered mountain and tundra
species at the Highland Wildlife Park

- Antlers Cafe
- Gift shop
- Free parking
- Play area
- Picnic Area
- Free guidebook
- Daily animal talks

Highland Wildlife Park
Kincraig, Kingussie.
(7 miles south of Aviemore)
Open daily from 10am.

tel: 01540 651 270
www.highlandwildlifepark.org

Cairngorm Walking Services

Walking at Revack
Visitor attraction set in 350 acres of outstanding scenery, Walled garden, Ornamental lochs, 10 miles of walks and trails, Garden centre, Gift shop and Restaurant. Rich in wildlife.

CairnGorm Mountain - Walking
CairnGorm Mountain offers a weekly programme of regular ranger guided walks for all ages and abilities and a number of spectacular night walks.
www.cairngormmountain.org.uk

Walking at Glenlivet
Lying between the Ladder and the Cromdale Hills in the Cairngorms National Park, the two broad straths of rivers Avon and Livet form the 23,000 hectare Glenlivet Estate, part of the Crown Estate. The Crown Estate welcomes visitors who wish to explore the Glenlivet Estate trails for walking, cycling and informal recreation.

Mountain Innovations Ltd.
Mountain Innovations, the Park's foremost mountain walking specialists, guarantees you fully qualified guides with an unrivalled knowledge of the mountain environment.
www.scotmountain.co.uk

Beallich Limited
Visit Scotlandbeallich is a health and activity provider with a fantastic location in the Haughs of Cromdale.
www.beallich.com

Forestry Commission Scotland
www.forestry.gov.uk/scotland

The Scottish Outdoor Access Code.
www.outdooraccess-scotland.com

G2
Based in Aviemore near Inverness in the Cairngorm National Park we are ideally placed to access a wide range of outdoor activities for all the family. Our highly experienced team of outdoor instructors cater for all ages
www.g2outdoor.co.uk

Active Outdoor Pursuits
Active offer walks tailored to suit all abilities from lowland walks to high-level mountain walks.
www.activeoutdoorpursuits.com

Extreme Dream
Indoor climbing centre with various climbing walls. We also have a large program of indoor and outdoor activities for everyone.
www.extreme-dream.com

Stick your own
picture here

Stick your own
picture here

Stick your own
picture here

Stick your own
picture here

Brooklynn Guest House

Location - **Grantown-on-Spey**
Make Brooklynn your base for a memorable walking holiday. Enjoying yourself can be tiring – so return to Brooklynn and relax. Have a delicious home cooked dinner, and maybe a wee malt, before retiring to your comfortable room to refresh yourself for yet another wonderful day.
Operating - February to October

Contact
tel (01479) 873113
www.woodier.com
brooklynn@woodier.com

★★★★

Ardselma Guest House

Location - **Kingussie**
Ardselma is a family run guesthouse offering bed and breakfast, dinner and packed lunches. Located only a few minutes walk from Kingussie Golf Club there are also numerous visitor attractions and activities nearby such as horse riding, hill walking, bird watching and much more. No dinners supplied. Open all year round.

Contact details:
tel 07786 696384
email: valerieardselma@aol.com

Dog Owners

Enjoy Your Walk
But remember you and your dog share the outdoors with others.

YOUR DOG DOESN'T KNOW ANY BETTER. MAKE SURE YOU DO.

Scotland's outdoors is a great place for dogs and owners. Walking the dog is good for your health and quality of life, as well as providing the simple pleasure of just being out and about. Remember too, you now have the right to be on most land for recreation providing you act responsibly (as set out in the Scottish Outdoor Access Code).

However, dogs that aren't kept under proper control can be a real concern for some people, including many land managers and visitors to the countryside. Dogs can worry and injure farm animals, disturb wildlife and alarm other people. Farmers also have concerns about dogs spreading diseases, especially if they've not been regularly wormed.

In using your access rights, you must keep your dog under proper control. This leaflet sets out your main responsibilities as a dog owner and advises on what proper control is in everyday situations. Please read it carefully and do what it recommends. Because let's face it, as much as you love them, your dog is a bit of a daftie when it comes to understanding the Scottish Outdoor Access Code.

Stick your own
picture here

Stick your own
picture here

Stick your own
picture here

Stick your own
picture here

silverglades
holiday homes

**NEW FOR 2009
Exclusive Silverglades
Select Range.**

Silverglades combines fine quality
accommodation with a high level of
Customer Service, and is set at the foot
of the Cairngorm Mountains in the
Cairngorms National Park.

Silverglades 33 holiday homes provides
the ideal holiday destination for people
of all ages, at any time of the year.

stylish self catering holidays
aviemore scotland

Silverglades
Dalnabay, Aviemore
Tel 01479 810165
www.silvergladesaviemore.co.uk

Dog Owners

9 POINTS TO HELP YOU TAKE THE LEAD

1) Don't take your dog into fields where there are lambs, calves or other young animals.

2) Don't take your dog into fields of vegetables or fruit unless you are on a clear path, such as a core path or right of way, but keep your dog to the path.

3) Never let your dog worry or attack farm animals.

4) If you go into a field of farm animals, keep as far as possible from the animals and keep your dog on a short lead or under close control.

5) If cattle react aggressively and move towards you, keep calm, let the dog go and take the shortest, safest route out of the field.

6) During the bird breeding season (usually April to July), keep your dog under close control or on a short lead in areas such as moorland, forests, grassland, loch shores and the seashore.

7) Pick up and remove your dog's faeces if it fouls in a public open place or where there is a risk to farming interests.

8) Some reservoirs and streams are used for public water supply. If there are intakes nearby, keep your dog out of the water.

9) In recreation areas and other public places, avoid causing concern to others by keeping your dog under close control.

Stick your own
picture here

Stick your own
picture here

Stick your own
picture here

Stick your own
picture here

Index

Angus Glens Walks   12, 16
Glendoll Forest Walk   22
Invermark Castle to Loch Lee   24
Invermark to Queens Well   26
Loch Brandy Walk   28
South Esk Loop & Trout Loch   30
South Esk River Walk   32
The Dounalt Walk   34
The Minister's Path   36
Walk up to Corrie Fee Reserve   38
White Water Trail   40

Aviemore & Glenmore   12, 50
Allt Mor All Abilities Trail   50
Allt Mor to Cairngorms   52
Aviemore Orbital Path   54
Aviemore Speyside Golf Walk   56
Aviemore to Boat of Garten   58
Coire Cas Lower Loop   60
Coylumbridge to the Iron Bridge   62
Craigellachie Nature Reserve Trails   64
Glenmore Forest Trail   66
Lilly Loch Walk   68
Loch an Eilein Trail Circular   70
Loch Morlich Circular   72
Loch nan Carriagen Stone Circle   74
Lochan Nan Nathrach Trail   76
Loch Vaa   78
Ryvoan & Green Loch Trex   80
The Queens Forest Walk   82
The Woodland Trail   84

Ballater, Braemar & Dinnet   12, 86
*Ballater Area Walks
Ballater Golf Course Walk   94
Craigendarroch Walk   96
Lock Muick End View Circular   98
Pannanich Woods   100
Seven Bridges Walk   102

*Braemar Area Walks
Around Craig Leek   104
Keiloch Crag   106
Morrone Birkwood   108
Morrone Hill Walk   110
Queen's Drive Walk   112
River Dee Walk   114
The Creag Choinnich Walk   116
The Lion's Face & Cromlins   118
*Dinnet Area Walks
Burn O'Vat Circular   120
Cambus O May Forest Trails   122
Cambus O May Bridge Walk   124
Glen Tanar Nature Reserve   126
Little Ord Circular   128
Loch Kinord Circular   130

**Boat of Garten, Carrbridge,
Grantown & Nethy Bridge**   3, 132
*Boat of Garten Area Walks
Boat of Garten to Carrbridge   142
Boat of Garten to Loch Vaa   144
Boat of Garten Riverside Walk   146
Boat of Garten Woodland Walks   148
Loch Garten & Garten Woods   150
*Carrbridge Area Walks
Carrbridge Circuit Trail   152
Carrbridge Woodland Trails   154
Docharn Woods Walk   156
Landmark Adventure Trails   158
Sluggan Bridge Walk   160
The Gurkha Bridge Walk   162
*Grantown-on-Spey Area Walks
Anagach Woods   164
General Wade's Military Road   166
Grantown-on-Spey River Walk   168
Kylintra Meadows   170
Revach Estate   172
The Blue Trail Beachen Woods   174

Scottish Outdoor Access Code

The outdoors is where land managers make a living. It is the home of Scotland's diverse wildlife and is enjoyed by the many people who live there and visit it. You can exercise access rights responsibly if you:

1. Take responsibility for your own actions;

2. Respect people's privacy and peace of mind. When close to a house or garden, keep a sensible distance from the house, use a path or track if there is one, and take extra care at night;

3. Help land managers and others to work safely and effectively . Do not hinder land management operations and follow advice from land managers. Respect requests for reasonable limitations on when and where you can go;

4. Care for your environment. Do not disturb wildlife, leave the environment as you find it and follow a path or track if there is one;

5. Keep your dog under proper control. Do not take it through fields of calves and lambs, and dispose of dog dirt;

6. Take extra care if you are organising an event or running a business and ask the land owner's advice.

Visit
www.outdooraccess-scotland.com

Index

Viewpoints Walk 176
Waterfall Walk 178
Nethy Bridge Area Walks
Broomhill River Walk 180
Castle Roy Loop 182
Lettoch Walk 184
Nethy Bridge Circuit 186
Nethy Bridge to Boat of Garten 188
Nethy Bridge Woodland Walks 190
Riverside & Dell Woods Walk 192
Wilderness Trail 194

Featured Walks at a Glance 12

Getting Around 10

Glenlivet / Tomintoul & Strathdon 14, 196

Glenlivet / Tomintoul Area Walks
Braes Heritage Trail 202
Bochel Circuit 204
Clash Wood 206
Drumin Circular & Castle 208
Geln Brown - Kylnadrochit 199
Glenconglass to Carn Daimh 212
Glenmulliach Nature Trail 214

Knock Earth House Walk 216
Tom Dubh Wood Walk 218
Tomnavoulin - Carn Daimh 220
Strathdon Area Walks Area Walks
Ben Newe Forest Trail 222
Introduction 4

Kincraig & Kingussie 15, 224
Kincraig Area Walks
Farleitter Crag & Ridge Walk 230
Feshiebridge Woodland Walk 232

Kincraig Speyside & Woods 234
River Feshie & Sculpture Trail 236
Loch Insh Interpretative Trail 238
The Duke of Gordon's Monument 240
Uath Lochans 242
Uath Lochans to Feshiebridge 244
Kingussie Area Walks
Birch Woodie 246
Creag Bheag - Loch Gynack
Insh Marshes 250
Jubilee Walk / Ruthven Barracks 252
Kingussie Golf Course Walk 254
Ruthven Barracks & Glen Tromie 256
Tom Baraidh Walk 258
West Terrace Circular 260

Laggan & Newtonmore 15, 262
Laggan Area Walks
Allt Mhoraich Trail 266
Blackwood & the Pictish Fort 268
Druim an Aird & Pattack Falls 270
Glen Truim Woods & View Point 272
Gorstean Crag Walk 274
Laggan River Spey Walk 276
Newtonmore Area Walks
Cat of 6 Trails 278
Highland Folk Museum Tour 280
Loch Imrich Walk 282
Wildcat Circular Trail 284

Walking Contacts & Services 312

Stick your own
picture here

Stick your own
picture here

Stick your own
picture here

Stick your own
picture here

Forestry Commission
Scotland

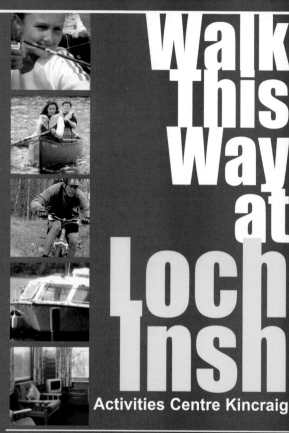

Walk This Way at Loch Insh

Activities Centre Kincraig

Walk, sail, ski, ride, play, fish and relax - you can do it
all at Loch Insh Centre in Kincraig. We also offer
wildlife boat tours across Loch Insh to see ospreys.

Accommodation, with a bar and waterside restaurant
on the banks of Loch Insh, gift shop, children's play
and interpretative trail with information boards..